# FEAST OF FLAVOURS
from the Vietnamese Kitchen

# FEAST OF FLAVOURS from the Vietnamese Kitchen

A STEP-BY-STEP CULINARY ADVENTURE

Nguyen Thanh Diep

Marshall Cavendish Cuisine

The Publisher wishes to thank **Barang Barang Pte Ltd** and **Lim's Arts and Living** for the loan and use of their tableware.

Editor: Selina Kuo
Designers: Geoslyn Lim & Benson Tan
Photographer: Sam Yeo
Food Preparation: Cheong Mee Siew

© 2005 Marshall Cavendish International (Asia) Private Limited

Published by Times Editions – Marshall Cavendish Cuisine
An imprint of Marshall Cavendish International (Asia) Private Limited
A member of Times Publishing Limited
Times Centre, 1 New Industrial Road, Singapore 536196
Tel: (65) 6213 9300    Fax: (65) 6285 4871
E-mail: te@sg.marshallcavendish.com
Online Bookstore: http://www.marshallcavendish.com/genref

Malaysian Office:
Marshall Cavendish (Malaysia) Sdn Bhd (3024-D)
(General & Reference Publishing)
(Formerly known as Federal Publications Sdn Berhad)
Times Subang, Lot 46, Persiaran Teknologi Subang
Subang Hi-Tech Industrial Park
Batu Tiga, 40000 Shah Alam
Selangor Darul Ehsan, Malaysia
Tel: (603) 5635 2191, 5628 6888    Fax: (603) 5635 2706
E-mail: cchong@my.marshallcavendish.com

All rights reserved.  No part of this publication may be reproduced, stored in a retrieval system
or transmitted, in any form or by any means, electronic, mechanical, photocopying,
recording or otherwise, without the prior permission of the copyright owner.

**Limits of Liability/Disclaimer of Warranty:** The Author and Publisher of this book have used their best efforts
in preparing this book. The Publisher makes no representation or warranties with respect to the contents of
this book and is not responsible for the outcome of any recipe in this book. While the Publisher has reviewed
each recipe carefully, the reader may not always achieve the results desired due to variations in ingredients,
cooking temperatures and individual cooking abilities. The Publisher shall in no event be liable for any loss of profit
or any other commercial damage, including but not limited to special, incidental, consequential, or other damages.

**National Library Board Singapore Cataloguing in Publication Data**

Nguyen Thanh Diep.
Feast of flavours from the Vietnamese kitchen : a step-by-step
culinary adventure / Nguyen Thanh Diep. – Singapore : Marshall
Cavendish Cuisine, c2005.
p. cm. – (Feast of flavours)
Includes index.
ISBN : 981-232-677-4

1. Cookery, Vietnamese. I. Title. II. Series: Feast of flavours

TX724.5.V5
641.59597 -- dc21        SLS2004149960

Printed in Singapore by Times Graphics Pte Ltd

## Introduction
- 6 Cooking Techniques
- 8 Cooking Utensils
- 12 Weights & Measures

## Starters
- 16 Fresh Spring Rolls
- 19 Deep-fried Spring Rolls
- 21 Hanoi Prawn Fritters
- 22 Prawn Paste on Sugar Cane
- 24 Beef Rolls
- 26 Fried Chicken Wings in Fish Sauce
- 28 Squid Cakes

## Soups & Salads
- 32 Vietnamese Sour Fish Soup
- 35 Pumpkin Soup with Coconut Milk
- 37 Green Mango Salad
- 38 Water Convolvulus Salad
- 40 Beef Salad
- 43 Chicken Salad with Polygonum Leaves

## Seafood
- 46 Fish and Pineapple Stew
- 49 Baked Crabs
- 51 Steamed Fish with Sugar Cane
- 52 Steamed Fish with Fermented Soy Beans
- 54 Stir-fried Minced Eel with Lemon Grass
- 57 Fried Crab in Tamarind Sauce
- 59 Prawns Sautéed with Pork Belly
- 60 Stuffed Squid

## Meat & Poultry
- 64 Fried Lemon Grass Chicken
- 67 Steamed Chicken with Spring Onions
- 69 Vietnamese Beef Stew
- 70 Beef on Fire
- 72 Beef Cooked in Vinegar
- 75 Steamed Minced Pork with Duck Eggs
- 77 Pork Stewed in Coconut Juice
- 78 Stir-fried Frog in Coconut Milk

## Rice & Noodles
- 82 Traditional Chicken Noodle Soup
- 85 Beef Noodles
- 87 Duck Noodle Soup
- 88 Crabmeat Noodle Soup
- 90 Duck Cooked in Fermented Bean Curd
- 93 Saigon Fish Congee
- 95 Quang Noodles
- 97 Eel Noodles

## Desserts
- 100 Peanut and Sago Dessert
- 103 Sweet Yam Dessert
- 105 Tapioca Cake
- 106 Fresh Aloe Vera with Green Bean Soup
- 108 Black-eyed Peas in Glutinous Rice

## Glossary & Index
- 112 Glossary of Ingredients
- 118 Index

# INTRODUCTION

## COOKING TECHNIQUES

Vietnamese cooking does not require knowledge of any special skill or complicated technique. Often the key lies in getting the freshest possible ingredients because many, especially vegetables, are eaten raw or lightly cooked. The reliance on natural flavours is considerable in Vietnamese cuisine. At other times, strong flavours are boldly brought together by a combination of the dish itself and the accompanying dipping sauce. Although on the side, the dipping sauce, like the raw salad, contributes greatly to the overall taste, texture and enjoyment of the dish. Consequently, much attention should be paid to the preparation of not only the main dish, but also the dipping sauce, as well as acquiring the freshest possible salad. The cook's achievement lies in ensuring all the flavours, however forward or subtle, mesh well together.

The main cooking techniques utilised in this book are boiling, stewing, steaming, stir-frying and deep-frying.

### Boiling

Seemingly the simplest of cooking methods, boiling in itself breaks down into different categories, including rapid boiling, slow boiling and prolonged boiling. Knowing when to employ what boiling method is important to achieving a successful dish. Turning up the heat to hurry the boiling process is often not the answer. Because noodles, especially rice noodles, figure prominently in Vietnamese cuisine, mastering the appropriate boiling method is crucial, whether for blanching the noodles or preparing the soup that bathes the noodles. Preparing the base stock for the soup, for instance, will require prolonged, rigorous boiling, especially if it is derived from bones. Rapid boiling for a few minutes is applied to ingredients such as tomato wedges or other such vegetables going into a soup. Such a method means that the tomato wedges will be cooked through and just softened but not yet falling apart from too much heat. Other ingredients, such as fish pieces for example, may require slow boiling. This is because the violent motions of rapid boiling will cause the fish pieces to break into bits in the soup. The rolling actions of a slow boil, on the other hand, are gentle enough for the fish pieces to accommodate, so they will cook through while remaining in whole pieces.

### Stewing
Stewing is a versatile cooking method and basically means that the solid ingredients will be cooked in plenty of liquid, enough liquid, in fact, to cover all of the solid ingredients in the cooking utensil. By the end of cooking time, which is relatively lengthy compared to a stir-fried dish, the stewing liquid would have reduced considerably to become thickened and flavourful. The slightly extended cooking process, however, means that the dish is guaranteed to be richly tasty, with the solid ingredients imparting to the liquid their individual flavours and then absorbing the combined product back.

Stewing is generally recommended for tougher cuts of meat and fairly hardy vegetables. Ingredients that collapse readily with heat are likely to disappear in a stew, disintegrating and dissolving into the stewing liquid. The Vietnamese tend to use coconut juice as the base for their stewing liquid. The sweetness in coconut juice is subtle, but goes a long way in bringing out and together the contrasting flavours of the solid ingredients.

### Steaming
Steaming is a technique that cooks food in its own juices, and in view of the Vietnamese preference to rely on natural flavours, it is no wonder that steaming is a repeatedly employed method of cooking. When food is steamed, it does not come into direct contact with heat. Instead, the water that is below the food boils to produce steam that is, in turn, trapped under a lid and heat from the collected steam is what surrounds and cooks the food.

If you do not have a wok and/or steamer, a large and deep cooking pot with a snug-fitting lid or dutch oven will do. Begin by pouring some water into the pot and then position a rack inside. Arrange the food to be steamed in a heatproof (flameproof) bowl or dish before bringing the pot of water to the boil. When the water is boiling, remove the lid and place the bowl or dish of ingredients onto the rack. Lastly, replace the lid and steam for the duration needed.

Be mindful of the liquid level in the pot; the water should never splash onto the food during rapid boiling. Conversely, add only boiling hot water to the pot should it become dry. Adding cold water will only ruin your dish as the then tepid water will take time to return to the boil, causing your dish to cook unevenly.

### Stir-frying
Stir-frying is a method of cooking that should not last longer than 10–15 minutes from beginning to end. The short cooking time of stir-frying is at once its merit and also its bane. A short cooking time also means that there is not a lot of room for error. To avoid the latter, however, could not be easier. Just make sure that all the ingredients for the dish you are about to stir-fry are fully prepared before you even turn on the heat. If you do not have a wok, a large skillet or frying pan will do. Remember also to heat the wok or pan up before adding the oil. No ingredient should enter the wok or pan until the oil is heated through.

Precisely that the ingredients do not get a lot of cooking time, it is useful to remember to cut meat and vegetables to smaller pieces. Meat especially should be no more than thin slices or small dice. Another thing to take note is that ingredients similar in nature — hard, medium and soft — should be grouped together and added to the wok at the same time. Hard ingredients like carrots take more time to cook and soften than soft ingredients like snow peas that collapse readily with heat. More often than not, meats enter the wok before vegetables, of which the harder ones first. Grouping your ingredients and adding them systematically to the wok or pan will certainly ensure that your stir-fried dish will not be unevenly cooked.

### Deep-frying
This method of cooking involves bathing ingredients in hot oil to cook. If the oil is not hot enough for deep-frying at the time of lowering in the food items, they will end up absorbing more oil than they should. The excess oil, despite draining on absorbent paper, is also likely to cause the fried items to become soggy upon cooling. Conversely, if the oil is too hot, then the food items will burn on the outside before they cook through inside.

It is generally acknowledged that 180°C (350°F) is the best temperature for deep-frying. Certainly, however, some recipes will call for higher temperatures. In those instances, be mindful of the type of cooking oil that you are using. Some cooking oils, such as peanut oil, have higher smoking temperatures than most others. What this means is that oils like peanut oil can be heated to higher temperatures before smoking and making your stove-top look like a barbeque pit.

Another thing to take note of is how many items you lower into the oil at any one time. Consider that you have appropriately heated the oil for deep-frying, but should you lower too many items to be deep-fried at once, you will cause the temperature of the oil to dip below the desired temperature. Again, deep-frying in insufficiently heated oil leads to excessively oily and eventually soggy food.

# COOKING UTENSILS

**Wok**

Woks were traditionally made wholly of heavy cast iron and always round-based, with two small, semi-circular handles at opposing ends. Handling such a wok requires not only considerable strength, but also care. This is because the handles, too, would have become hot from cooking and kitchen towels or, more recently, oven gloves would be required to remove the wok from the stove.

With time and advancing technology, woks have since been made from aluminium and stainless steel and also changed slightly in shape and form; some woks are flat-based to accommodate electric hobs. The popularity and convenience of non-stick cooking surfaces has since also extended itself to some woks. A key advantage of woks made of lighter materials, such as aluminium, is that they are easier to handle. Some of the more modern woks have long plastic handles that can be safely held when cooking. Older woks of the kind tended to have wooden handles that can become unhygienic over time because of their porous surfaces. Electric woks are generally avoided in Asian kitchens.

When choosing a wok for yourself, be mindful of your needs and kitchen conditions over the look and base-material of the utensil. If you have a gas hob, for instance, then a round-based wok will rest more securely on the metal frame of the hob than one flat-based. This takes into account how the action of stir-frying can cause a flat-based wok to slide along the metal frame and away from the heat source or, worse, topple. Also, there may arise a situation where you feel that you prefer one base-material's properties over another, e.g. you would choose stainless steel over aluminium, but if the stainless steel wok is heavier than you would have liked, then choose the lighter, aluminium wok. A wok that feels heavy in the store will most certainly be twice as heavy at home when filled with ingredients and, not to mention, a hazard over heat.

In selecting a wok, size definitely outweighs all other considerations. If you frequently cook for between two and four people, then a small- to medium-sized wok is ideal. Using a wok larger than what is needed will only give you less control over the food you are cooking. Remember that a larger wok means a larger base, which is where most of the heat is conducted, so cooking few ingredients in a large wok will definitely dry out the dish in a very short time. Cooking the same amount of food in a smaller, more appropriately sized wok means that some of the ingredients will always fall to the sides in the process of stir-frying, thus removing them from direct, intense heat all of the time. Conversely, if you find yourself cooking a lot of ingredients in a small wok, then the repercussions are that the dish will be unevenly cooked. Ingredients distributed high along the sides of the wok are likely to be undercooked, while those trapped in the centre will cook from steam heat rather than contact with the wok's metal surface. This is because the ingredients below those in the centre are nearer to the base of the wok, and when they cook, the moisture they contain turns into steam that rises and cooks the ingredients above without the browning they require.

Cast iron woks, although not non-stick and heavy, are still preferred in many Asian households. This is because they are relatively inexpensive and can withstand daily doses of intensely high heat for years without warping. The same cannot be said for woks made of other materials. Cooking in a cast iron wok over high heat also imparts an inimitable smoky flavour the Cantonese call *wok hei* or "wok fragrance" to a dish.

### Clay pot

Clay pots today come in many shapes and sizes. For cooking, the type of clay pot most commonly used is wide-mouthed and has one stubby handle or two even shorter handles at opposing ends. Clay pots require very careful handling because they crack easily, and once cracked, they can no longer be used over the stove. In a bid to overcome their delicate nature, some makers of clay pots reinforce each pot with a wire mesh woven around the sides and bottom, while others glaze their pots both inside and out. Most clay pots, however, have only their interiors glazed.

One advantage of cooking with a clay pot is that it retains heat long after it is transferred from the stove to the table. The clay pot, while taking some time to heat up in the beginning, is also a very even conductor of heat, making it the ideal utensil for stews or other dishes that require prolonged and even distribution of low to medium heat.

### Steamboat

The steamboat is what some Asians call a hot pot. A steamboat or hot pot experience consists of a pot of stock kept steaming or boiling hot at the centre of a table for diners to cook their selections of the raw ingredients provided on the side. Such a setup gives diners full control over the degree of doneness of their food.

Traditional steamboats have a funnel in the centre and what seems like a moat surrounding it. For a hot pot experience, hot charcoal pieces would be placed below the "moat" and inside the funnel to keep the stock in the "moat" hot. With time, charcoal-fuelled steamboats gave way to electric steamboats, many of which look no different from a wide and shallow cooking pot with an electric cord attached. The beauty of the latter is that the heat never runs out.

### Spatula

The spatula is the instrument that the cook uses to stir, flip and manoeuvre ingredients in a wok. Spatulas can be made of metal, wood or plastic, and the material to choose really depends on the type of wok it will be used against. Generally, non-stick surfaces will require plastic or wooden spatulas to prevent scratches or similar damage to the non-stick coating. Metal spatulas, then, are better suited to cast iron or stainless steel woks. Most importantly, however, the spatula should feel like an extension of the cook's arm, in that it should feel comfortable and aid rather than hinder the movement of ingredients in the given wok. Left-handed people, for example, are more aware that some spatulas, as is the case with other kitchen utensils such as peelers, feel more cumbersome than others.

### Steamer

Into the twenty-first century, steamers come in different shapes and sizes. The basic, multi-tiered form with a lid on top, however, remains unchanged. The most traditional would be bamboo steamers, which are also the cheapest option. Bamboo steamers can be used in conjuction with any round-based wok. Just ensure that water in the wok does not surge past the base of the bottom tier upon boiling.

By comparison, aluminium steamers have a couple of advantages. First, the metal used to make the steamers mean that they are relatively inexpensive, durable and completely safe from mould-growth, which tends to affect bamboo steamers over time. Second, aluminium steamers can be used directly over stove-top heat because they each come with a bottom pan for water, and on top of the bottom pan are stacked several perforated tiers and then the lid. Steam from the water in the bottom pan will rise and move freely through all the tiers because of the holes cut into the base of each tier and be trapped by the lid right on top.

Today, there is also the electric steamer. A modern appliance like the deep-fryer, the electric steamer is essentially an electric kettle with the body of a steamer. Made mostly of plastic, the electric steamer consists of a bottom pan, a number of tiers and a lid. The bottom pan, in this instance, is fitted with an electric heating apparatus.

## Mortar and pestle

The mortar and pestle is useful in breaking down small quantities of ingredients such as roasted skinned peanuts and leafy herbs. The mortar and pestle also allows the cook total control over the ultimate texture of the pounded ingredients, which can range from coarse to very fine. Neither quality, that of being able to handle small quantities or that of being able to control the texture, is something that the standard blender (processor) can imitate.

## Cleaver

A sharp cleaver is probably the most useful utensil one could own in an Asian, and possibly non-Asian, kitchen. This is because the added height and weight of the cleaver, as compared to a standard carving knife, can serve a great number of other purposes. The added weight of the cleaver, for example, facilitates the application of enough force to cut through bones, whether to produce poultry joints, large fish steaks, or serving-size spare ribs. For the same reason, the back of the cleaver can be used as a meat mallet and the side of the cleaver can be used to smash certain ingredients, such as peeled ginger and garlic, until fine in one swift motion, thereby relieving the cook from having to mince them. Even for an ingredient as fragile as silken bean curd, the cleaver is the utensil of choice. In halving a piece of bean curd lengthways, for example, the cleaver allows the cook to at once cut through, as well as provide support for and lift the upper half, altogether minimising damage to both halves.

Despite its size, which makes it appear more menacing, the cleaver is actually safer than the standard carving knife when there is a lot of repetitive chopping or slicing to do. This is because the side of the cleaver can be propped against the curled fingers of the opposing hand to guide the cutting edge, so the chances of slipping and accidentally injuring parts of the opposing hand are considerably lowered. The side of the cleaver is also excellent for transferring prepared ingredients from the chopping board to wherever it is needed, whether a plate for later use or straight to the cooking utensil.

## Wire strainer

Traditional wire strainers have woven brass wire attached to long bamboo handles. Such strainers are better suited to use with woks because of the wide angle at which the mesh baskets are attached to the handles. These strainers can be used to blanch noodles or vegetables in hot water or drain deep-fried items from hot oil.

The more modern wire strainers appear like elongated sieves attached to relatively shorter and vertical handles. These strainers are more convenient because they can be lowered straight down into a normal cooking pot, but they also serve no other purpose aside from blanching.

# WEIGHTS & MEASURES

Quantities for this book are given in Metric and American (spoon and cup) measures. Standard spoon and cup measurements used are: 1 teaspoon = 5 ml, 1 dessertspoon = 10 ml, 1 tablespoon = 15 ml, 1 cup = 250 ml. All measures are level unless otherwise stated.

## DRY MEASURES

| Metric | Imperial |
|---|---|
| 30 grams | 1 ounce |
| 45 grams | 1½ ounces |
| 55 grams | 2 ounces |
| 70 grams | 2½ ounces |
| 85 grams | 3 ounces |
| 100 grams | 3½ ounces |
| 110 grams | 4 ounces |
| 125 grams | 4½ ounces |
| 140 grams | 5 ounces |
| 280 grams | 10 ounces |
| 450 grams | 16 ounces (1 pound) |
| 500 grams | 1 pound, 1½ ounces |
| 700 grams | 1½ pounds |
| 800 grams | 1¾ pounds |
| 1 kilogram | 2 pounds, 3 ounces |
| 1.5 kilograms | 3 pounds, 4½ ounces |
| 2 kilograms | 4 pounds, 6 ounces |

## LENGTH

| Metric | Imperial |
|---|---|
| 0.5 cm | ¼ inch |
| 1 cm | ½ inch |
| 1.5 cm | ¾ inch |
| 2.5 cm | 1 inch |

## LIQUID AND VOLUME MEASURES

| Metric | Imperial | American |
|---|---|---|
| 5 ml | ⅙ fl oz | 1 teaspoon |
| 10 ml | ⅓ fl oz | 1 dessertspoon |
| 15 ml | ½ fl oz | 1 tablespoon |
| 60 ml | 2 fl oz | ¼ cup (4 tablespoons) |
| 85 ml | 2½ fl oz | ⅓ cup |
| 90 ml | 3 fl oz | ⅜ cup (6 tablespoons) |
| 125 ml | 4 fl oz | ½ cup |
| 180 ml | 6 fl oz | ¾ cup |
| 250 ml | 8 fl oz | 1 cup |
| 300 ml | 10 fl oz (½ pint) | 1¼ cups |
| 375 ml | 12 fl oz | 1½ cups |
| 435 ml | 14 fl oz | 1¾ cups |
| 500 ml | 16 fl oz | 2 cups |
| 625 ml | 20 fl oz (1 pint) | 2½ cups |
| 750 ml | 24 fl oz (1⅕ pints) | 3 cups |
| 1 litre | 32 fl oz (1⅗ pints) | 4 cups |
| 1.25 litres | 40 fl oz (2 pints) | 5 cups |
| 1.5 litres | 48 fl oz (2⅖ pints) | 6 cups |
| 2.5 litres | 80 fl oz (4 pints) | 10 cups |

## OVEN TEMPERATURE

| Regulo | °C | °F | Gas |
|---|---|---|---|
| Very slow | 120 | 250 | 1 |
| Slow | 150 | 300 | 2 |
| Moderately slow | 160 | 325 | 3 |
| Moderate | 180 | 350 | 4 |
| Moderately hot | 190/200 | 370/400 | 5/6 |
| Hot | 210/220 | 410/440 | 6/7 |
| Very hot | 230 | 450 | 8 |
| Super hot | 250/290 | 475/550 | 9/10 |

## ABBREVIATION

| | |
|---|---|
| Tbsp | tablespoon |
| dsp | dessertspoon |
| tsp | teaspoon |
| kg | kilogram |
| g | gram |
| l | litres |
| ml | mililitres |

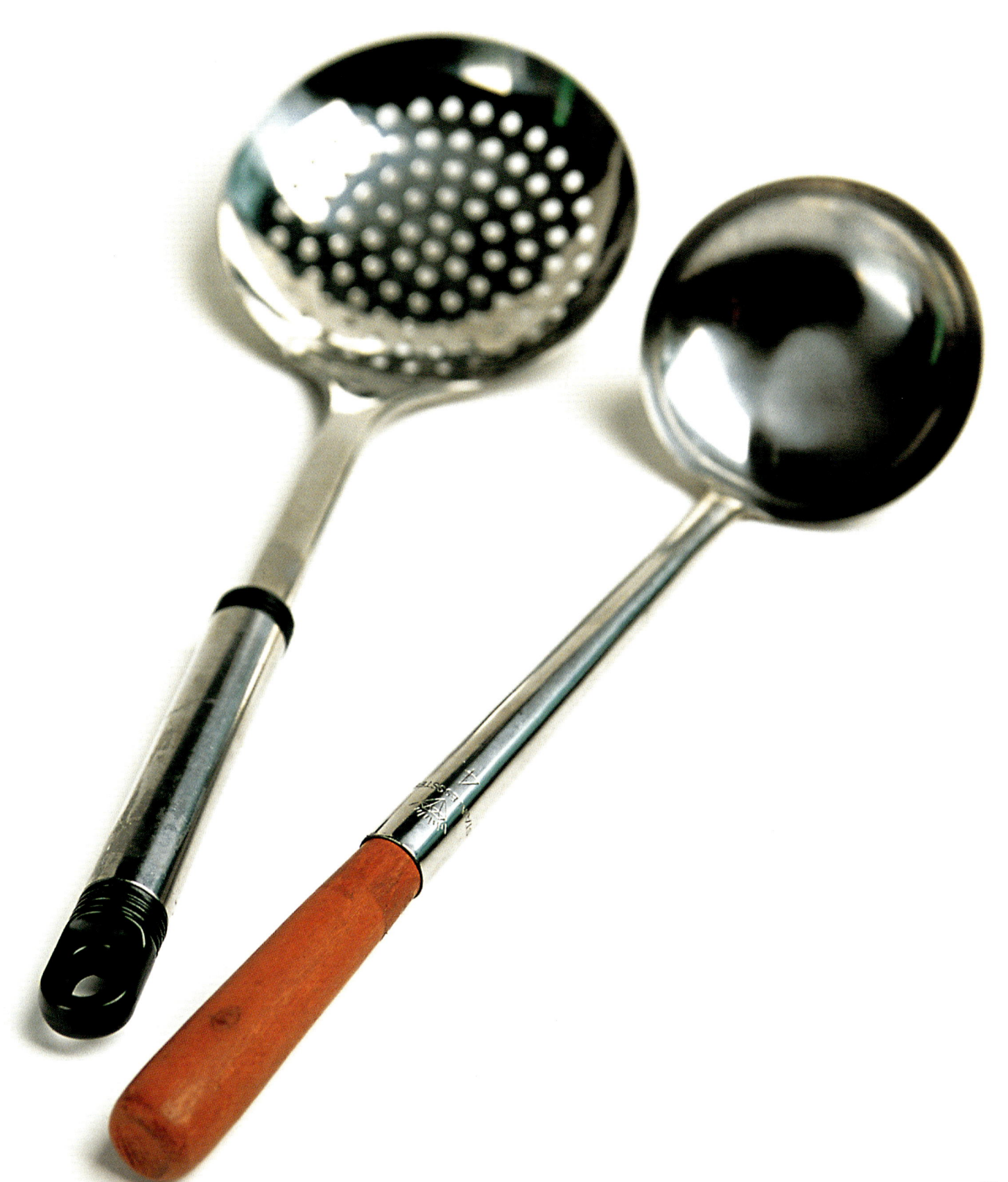

# STARTERS

Fresh Spring Rolls
Deep-fried Spring Rolls
Hanoi Prawn Fritters
Prawn Paste on Sugar Cane
Beef Rolls
Fried Chicken Wings in Fish Sauce
Squid Cakes

Carefully slice off stems of Chinese lettuce leaves. Removing the hard stems makes for easier rolling later.

Holding pork, prawns, and chive in place, carefully fold lower edge of rice paper over. Dampened rice paper is sticky and difficult to undo.

To keep the dipping sauce for future use, bring sauce to the boil and cool before refrigerating. Sauce can be stored for up to a week and served cold.

*Step-By-Step*

# FRESH SPRING ROLLS

The combination of Chinese lettuce, mint leaves and garlic chives gives this Vietnamese classic an unmistakeably light and fresh taste.

### Ingredients

| | |
|---|---|
| Round rice papers | 30 sheets, 20 cm (8 inches) in diameter |
| Warm boiled water | as required |
| Chinese lettuce leaves | 300 g (10½ oz), washed and drained |
| Mint leaves | 50 g (2 oz), washed and stalks discarded |
| Fresh rice vermicelli | 1 kg (2 lb 3 oz), replaceable with Indian string hoppers (*putu mayam*) or thick round rice (*laksa*) noodles |
| Garlic (Chinese) chives | 200 g (7 oz), washed and cut into 12-cm (5-inch) lengths |
| Lean pork | 300 g (10½ oz), boiled for 15 minutes or until cooked then thinly sliced |
| Freshwater prawns (shrimps) | 500 g (1 lb 1½ oz), boiled and peeled |

### Dipping Sauce (combined)

| | |
|---|---|
| Preserved soy bean paste | 5 Tbsp |
| Coconut juice | 2 Tbsp |
| Chopped lemon grass | 1 Tbsp |
| Light soy sauce | 1 Tbsp |
| Skinned peanuts (groundnuts) | 2 Tbsp, pounded |
| Sugar | 2 tsp |
| Minced chilli | 2 tsp |
| Minced garlic | 2 tsp |

### Method

- Lay 1 sheet of rice paper on a round tray or plate. Smear on warm, boiled water to soften.
- Put 1 lettuce leaf and 1 mint leaf at lower end of rice paper, followed by some rice vermicelli on top.
- Fold in left and right sides of rice paper, resulting length should be about 10 cm (4 inches).
- Position 1 chive stalk along length of roll, leaving about 2 cm (1 inch) to stick out on 1 side.
- Put 1 piece of pork and 2 prawns on top of other ingredients, then roll up firmly. Dampened rice paper will stick to seal.
- Repeat process until ingredients are used up. Serve rolls with dipping sauce.

# DEEP-FRIED SPRING ROLLS

The Vietnamese version of a familiar favourite the world over is richly stuffed with pork, crabmeat, yam and black fungus for crunch.

### Ingredients
| | |
|---|---|
| Minced pork | 300 g (10½ oz) |
| Crabmeat | 300 g (10½ oz), coarsely chopped and mashed, or minced prawn (shrimp) meat |
| Yam (taro) | 300 g (10½ oz), washed, peeled and finely shredded |
| Dried black (wood ear) fungus | 5, soaked to soften and finely shredded |
| Minced shallots | 2 tsp |
| Minced garlic | 1 tsp |
| Round rice papers | 30 sheets, 15 cm (6 inches) in diameter |
| Coconut juice | 125 ml (4 fl oz / ½ cup) |
| Cooking oil | 500 ml (16 fl oz / 2 cups) |
| Chinese lettuce leaves | |
| Mint leaves | |

### Seasoning
| | |
|---|---|
| Chicken seasoning powder | 4 tsp |
| Ground black pepper | 1 tsp |
| Salt | 2 tsp |

### Dipping Sauce (combined)
| | |
|---|---|
| Fish sauce | 1 Tbsp |
| Coconut juice | 2 Tbsp, or boiled water |
| Sugar | 1 tsp |
| Vinegar | 1 Tbsp, or lemon juice |
| Garlic | 1 clove, peeled and minced |
| Red chilli (optional) | 1 or to taste, minced |

## Step-By-Step

After coarsely chopping crabmeat, mash with a fork until fine.

Put all stuffing ingredients — pork crabmeat, yam, black fungus, shallots and garlic — into a bowl and mix well.

To prevent the rolls from sticking together when cooking, lower them into hot oil 1 by 1 and have no more than 2 or 3 rolls in the oil at one time.

### Method
- Prepare stuffing. Combine pork, crabmeat, yam, black fungus, shallots and garlic in a large bowl. Mix in seasoning ingredients. Set aside.
- Lay 1 sheet of rice paper on a round tray. Smear on coconut juice to soften. Put 1 Tbsp stuffing onto lower end of rice paper. Then, fold in left and right sides and roll up firmly. Each roll should be 3–4 cm (1½–2 inches) long. Repeat process until ingredients are used up.
- Heat oil in a wok or deep-fryer. Deep-fry spring rolls over medium heat until golden brown.
- Serve hot with some lettuce and mint leaves, as well as dipping sauce.

# HANOI PRAWN FRITTERS

Traditionally, prawns for the dish were not peeled because of the calcium the shells contained. The shells also help maintain crispness.

### Ingredients
| | |
|---|---|
| Prawns (shrimps) | 1 kg (2 lb 3 oz), small (50–60 pieces), washed |
| Limes | as required |
| Water | as required |
| Potatoes | 500 g (1 lb 1½ oz), peeled, washed and julienned |
| Cooking oil | 500 ml (16 fl oz / 2 cups) |
| Chinese lettuce leaves (optional) | 100 g (3½ oz), washed and drained well |
| Mint leaves (optional) | 100 g (3½ oz), washed and drained well |

### Batter
| | |
|---|---|
| Eggs | 3 |
| Plain (all-purpose) flour | 500 g (1 lb 1½ oz) |
| Rice flour | 250 g (9 oz) |
| Turmeric powder | 2 tsp |
| Chicken seasoning powder | 4 tsp |
| Salt | 2 tsp |
| Hot water | as required |

### Dipping Sauce (combined)
| | |
|---|---|
| Fish sauce | 1 Tbsp |
| Coconut juice | 2 Tbsp, or boiled water |
| Sugar | 1 tsp |
| Vinegar | 1 Tbsp, or lemon juice |
| Garlic | 1 clove, peeled and minced |
| Red chilli (optional) | 1 or to taste, minced |

## Step-By-Step

To julienne, first thinly slice peeled potatoes, then stack slices up and slice into shreds.

Make enough lime water to soak potato shreds completely. The shreds will not discolour as a result.

Beat batter ingredients together until smooth and consistency is similar to that of condensed milk.

## Method

- Peel prawns if desired, but leave tails intact.
- Make sufficient lime water to soak julienned potatoes until required. To make lime water, squeeze the juice of 1 lime into 1 litre (4 cups / 1³⁄₅ pints) water, increasing proportionately.
- Prepare batter. In a bowl, beat eggs, then mix in flours. Add turmeric powder, seasoning powder and salt, then continue to beat until mixture becomes smooth. Add some hot water if the mixture is too thick.
- Combine batter, prawns and drained potato shreds in a larger bowl.
- Heat oil in a wok or skillet (frying pan). Use a ladle to scoop batter (containing at least 2 prawns and some potato shreds) to lower into hot oil. Make sure that fritters do not stick together while frying. Cook until golden brown.
- Serve fritters with dipping sauce. For a lighter experience, eat fritters with some lettuce and mint leaves.

Slice lard into 1.5-cm (3/4-inch) wide pieces, then slice across into smaller pieces.

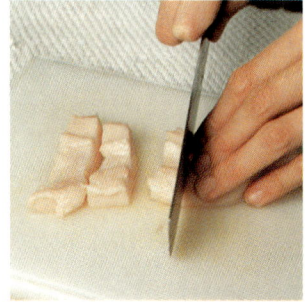

Using a sharp cleaver, peel and quarter each sugar cane stick by hacking down like firewood. Then, pare down 90° edge to make more rounded.

For easier handling of prawn paste, first wet hands to prevent sticking, then wrap 1 Tbsp paste around sugar cane length.

*Step-By-Step*

# PRAWN PASTE ON SUGAR CANE

Succulent prawn meat on lengths of sweet sugar cane are bound to delight both the family and guests.

### Ingredients

| | |
|---|---|
| Prawns (shrimps) | 1 kg (2 lb 3 oz) |
| Sugar cane | 5 sticks, each 10 cm (4 inch), washed and peeled |
| Lard | 100 g (3½ oz), washed and cut into 1.5-cm (3/4-inch) wide pieces |
| Sugar | 3 tsp |
| Garlic | 10 cloves, peeled |
| Salt | 1 tsp |

### Dipping Sauce (combined)

| | |
|---|---|
| Fish sauce | 1 Tbsp |
| Coconut juice | 2 Tbsp, or boiled water |
| Sugar | 1 tsp |
| Vinegar | 1 Tbsp, or lemon juice |
| Garlic | 1 clove, peeled and minced |
| Red chilli (optional) | 1 or to taste, minced |

### Method

- Wash, peel and devein prawns. Set aside.
- Quarter each sugar cane piece lengthways, then pare the pointed edge down to make rounder.
- Combine lard and sugar in an ovenproof (flameproof) bowl, then leave in oven preheated to 120°C/250°F for about 30 minutes.
- In the meantime, blend (process) prawns and garlic together until well mixed.
- In a bowl, combine prawn paste and lard, then add salt.
- Take 1 Tbsp paste and press around central portion of a sugar cane length, covering roughly two-thirds of stick. Repeat until ingredients are used up.
- Deep-fry, barbeque or oven grill prepared sugar cane lengths.
- Serve with dipping sauce or bottled chilli sauce.

Brandy not only imparts flavour to the beef slices, but also tenderises them.

Roll up beef slice with moderate firmness. If too loose, the roll will fall apart. If too tight, the filling will squeeze out on either side.

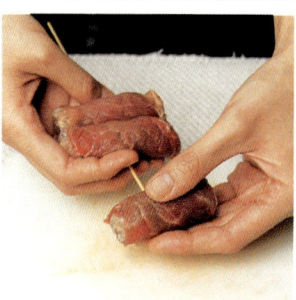

When poking beef rolls onto skewers, be mindful to poke through the outer ends of the slices so as to secure.

*Step-By-Step*

# BEEF ROLLS

Deeply aromatic and rich with meat juices, this starter will please any meat-lover.

### Ingredients
| | |
|---|---|
| Beef fillet | 1 kg (2 lb 3 oz) |
| Brandy | 1 tsp |
| Lean pork or chicken breast | 450 g (16 oz / 1 lb), minced |
| Crabmeat | 100 g (3½ oz) |
| Straw mushrooms | 200 g (7 oz), finely chopped |
| Cooking oil | 2 Tbsp |
| Chinese lettuce leaves | 300 g (10½ oz), washed and drained |

### Seasoning
| | |
|---|---|
| Chicken seasoning powder | 4 tsp |
| Ground white pepper | 1 tsp |
| Salt | 1 tsp |

### Dipping Sauce (combined)
| | |
|---|---|
| Fish sauce | 1 Tbsp |
| Coconut juice | 2 Tbsp, or boiled water |
| Sugar | 1 tsp |
| Vinegar | 1 Tbsp, or lemon juice |
| Garlic | 1 clove, peeled and minced |
| Red chilli (optional) | 1 or to taste, minced |

### Method
- Cut beef into thin slices, about 3 x 6 cm (1½ x 3 inches). When done, put beef slices in a bowl and add brandy. Mix and set aside for 30 minutes.
- Prepare filling. Combine minced pork or chicken, crabmeat and mushrooms in a bowl. Mix in seasoning ingredients and set aside.
- Heat cooking oil in a skillet (frying pan). Add filling and stir-fry for 10 minutes or until meat is cooked. Dish out and leave to cool for about 10 minutes.
- Put about 2 tsp filling onto a beef slice and roll up firmly. Repeat until beef slices are used up.
- Poke 3–4 rolls onto a skewer and grill them over charcoal heat. The rolls should be cooked after 10 minutes of grilling or when they turn golden on the outside. Alternatively, bake in oven preheated to 160°C/325°F for about 8 minutes, turning once or twice.
- Remove rolls from skewers and put on serving plate. Serve rolls with lettuce. To eat, wrap each beef roll with a lettuce leaf, then eat with dipping sauce.

Using a sharp carving knife or a cleaver, cut each chicken wing into 2 pieces.

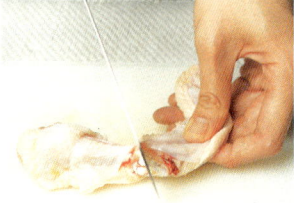

Combine all dipping sauce ingredients in a small mixing bowl. Increase quantities proportionately if more is needed.

Heat fish sauce through before adding sugar and turning down heat to cook until sugar is completely dissolved and liquid is thick. Stir contstantly.

# FRIED CHICKEN WINGS IN FISH SAUCE

A favourite of many, deep-fried chicken wings here are given a Vietnamese twist.

### Ingredients

| | |
|---|---|
| Chicken wings | 1 kg (2 lb 3 oz), washed and each cut into 2 pieces |
| Minced garlic | 3 tsp |
| Chicken seasoning powder | 3 tsp |
| Salt | 1/2 tsp |
| Cooking oil | 500 ml (16 fl oz / 2 cups) |
| Fish sauce | 125 ml (4 fl oz / 1/2 cup) |
| Sugar | 1 1/2 Tbsp |

### Dipping Sauce (combined)

| | |
|---|---|
| Lime juice | 1 Tbsp |
| Salt | 2 tsp |
| Ground black pepper | 1 tsp |

### Method

- Season chicken wings with minced garlic, seasoning powder and salt. Set aside for 30 minutes.
- Heat oil in a wok or deep-fryer. Add chicken wings and deep-fry over medium heat until golden brown. Drain.
- In a wok or cooking pan, cook fish sauce and sugar over low heat until sugar is completely dissolved and liquid thickens.
- Add fried chicken wings to thickened fish sauce and mix well. When wings are well coated with sauce, remove from heat.
- Transfer sauce-coated wings to a serving plate. Serve with dipping sauce.

To clean the blender (food processor) of sticky squid paste, use some salted water.

Flatten each squid ball by pressing down with the palm, not fingers, to minimise sticking and for a smoother finish.

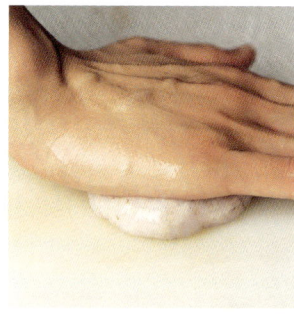

Remove as much excess oil from fried squid cakes as possible by draining on several changes of absorbent kitchen paper before serving.

*Step-By-Step*

# SQUID CAKES

Delight in the tastier relative of fish cakes, especially when eaten with lettuce and mint leaves and a sweet-and-sour dipping sauce.

### Ingredients
| | |
|---|---|
| Squids | 1 kg (2 lb 3 oz), washed, cleaned and skinned |
| Minced garlic | ½ tsp |
| Minced shallot | 1 tsp |
| Green (mung) bean powder | ½ tsp |
| Cooking oil | 125 ml (4 fl oz / ½ cup) |
| Chinese lettuce leaves | 200 g (7 oz), washed and drained |
| Mint leaves | as required |

### Seasoning
| | |
|---|---|
| Chicken seasoning powder | 3 tsp |
| Ground white pepper | 1 tsp |
| Sugar | 1 tsp |
| Salt | 1 tsp |

### Dipping Sauce (combined)
| | |
|---|---|
| Fish sauce | 1 Tbsp |
| Coconut juice | 2 Tbsp, or boiled water |
| Sugar | 1 tsp |
| Vinegar | 1 Tbsp, or lemon juice |
| Garlic | 1 clove, peeled and minced |
| Red chilli (optional) | 1 or to taste, minced |

### Method

- Cut squid tubes into small pieces. Blend (process) squid pieces to a fine paste. Transfer to a mixing bowl.
- Season squid paste with minced garlic and shallot, as well as seasoning ingredients.
- Shape squid paste into balls about 5 cm (2 inches) in diameter. Flatten them into round-shaped patties about 0.5-cm (¼-inch) thick.
- Heat oil in a wok or skillet (frying pan). Cook squid patties until golden brown.
- For presentation, cut squid cakes into diamond shapes and arrange on a plate. Garnish as desired with leaves and squid-cake trimmings.
- Serve squid cakes with lettuce and mint leaves, as well as dipping sauce.

Vietnamese Sour Fish Soup
Pumpkin Soup with Coconut Milk
Green Mango Salad
Water Convolvulus Salad
Beef Salad
Chicken Salad with Polygonum Leaves

SOUPS & SALADS

Use only a sharp carving knife or cleaver to make cuts on fish. A blunt instrument will cause unsightly jagged cuts.

After dissolving tamarind pulp in hot water by stirring, strain liquid for tamarind juice.

Add pineapple and vegetables only after the soup has been satisfactorily adjusted to taste because they cannot stand to be overcooked.

# VIETNAMESE SOUR FISH SOUP

Brightly colourful and appetisingly tangy, this nutritious soup of fish, pineapple and vegetables is full of crunch and a pleasure to the senses.

### Ingredients

| | |
|---|---|
| Mackerel | 1, about 1 kg (2 lb 3 oz), replaceable with mudfish (snakehead) or other freshwater fish |
| Pork stock | from boiling 300 g (10½ oz) pork bones in 1 litre (4 cups / 1⅗ pints) water for 1–2 hours |
| Salt | 1 tsp or to taste |
| Tamarind juice | from stirring 20 g (¾ oz) tamarind pulp in 250 ml (8 fl oz / 1 cup) hot water and then strained |
| Pineapple | ½, peeled, quartered lengthways then cut across into 0.5-cm (¼-inch) thick slices |
| Tomatoes | 2, each cut into 8 wedges |
| Bean sprouts | 50 g (2 oz), tailed |
| Chinese celery | 50 g (2 oz), leaves separated and stems cut into 3-cm (1½-inch) lengths |
| Minced garlic | 1 tsp, crisp-fried |
| Fish sauce | 2 Tbsp |
| Red chilli slices | 2 Tbsp |

### Seasoning

| | |
|---|---|
| Chicken seasoning powder | ½ tsp |
| Fish sauce | ½ tsp |
| Sugar | ½ tsp |

### Method

- Wash and clean fish. Make 3 diagonal cuts on each side of body. Set aside.
- Bring stock to the boil. Season with salt. Add fish and allow liquid to return to the boil, then add tamarind juice. Regularly remove scum from liquid surface.
- When fish is almost cooked, add seasoning ingredients. The soup should taste a bit sour and sweet. Adjust soup to taste, then add pineapple and tomato pieces, bean sprouts and Chinese celery stems. Return liquid to the boil before removing from heat.
- Transfer all or a portion of fish soup to a serving bowl, then garnish with fried garlic and Chinese celery leaves.
- Serve fish soup with fish sauce in a small saucer and chilli slices in another.

# PUMPKIN SOUP WITH COCONUT MILK

Sweet pumpkin, creamy coconut milk, and tiny but pungent dried prawns combine to produce a richly flavoured soup.

### Ingredients

| | |
|---|---|
| Coconut milk | 300 ml (10 fl oz / 1¼ cups) |
| Water | 800 ml (26 fl oz / 3¼ cups) |
| Dried prawns (shrimps) | 50 g (2 oz), soaked in warm water for 15 minutes then drained well and roughly pounded |
| Pumpkin | 1 kg (2 lb 3 oz), peeled and cut into bite-sized pieces |
| Straw mushrooms | 300 g (10½ oz) |
| Soft bean curd cubes | 20, each 5 x 5 cm (2 x 2 inches), deep-fried |
| Chicken seasoning powder | 3 tsp |
| Salt | 2 tsp |
| Ground black pepper | 2 tsp |

## Step-By-Step

Use a mortar and pestle to pound ready soaked dried prawns.

Drain soft bean curd pieces of excess liquid well before lowering into hot oil to avoid splattering.

The golden skin that forms with deep-frying bean curd not only adds texture to the ingredient, but also prevents it from breaking into bits.

### Method

- Bring coconut milk and water to the boil. Add dried prawns and pumpkin pieces. Cook for 10 minutes over medium heat.
- Add mushrooms and fried bean curd pieces. Cook for 5 minutes more. Then, season with seasoning powder and salt.
- Transfer soup into a large serving bowl and sprinkle on pepper.
- Serve with steamed rice.

# GREEN MANGO SALAD

Also known as Vietnamese mint, polygonum leaves impart an intense and inimitable aroma that uniquely brings out the flavour of prawns.

## Ingredients

| | |
|---|---|
| Green mangoes | 1 kg (2 lb 3 oz), peeled, seeds discarded and flesh julienned |
| Prawns (shrimps) | 300 g (10$\frac{1}{2}$ oz), barbecued or grilled and then peeled but with tails intact |
| Polygonum (*laksa*) leaves | 20 g ($\frac{3}{4}$ oz), stalks discarded and leaves coarsely chopped |
| Skinned peanuts (groundnuts) | 50 g (2 oz), roasted and coarsely pounded |
| Prawn (shrimp) crackers | 20, deep-fried |

### Dressing (combined)

| | |
|---|---|
| Chilli sauce | 4 Tbsp |
| Sugar | 3 Tbsp or more to taste |
| Light soy sauce | 2 Tbsp |

### Dipping Sauce (combined)

| | |
|---|---|
| Fish sauce | 1 Tbsp |
| Coconut juice | 2 Tbsp, or boiled water |
| Sugar | 1 tsp |
| Vinegar | 1 Tbsp, or lemon juice |
| Garlic | 1 clove, peeled and minced |
| Red chilli (optional) | 1 or to taste, minced |

## Step-By-Step

Cut top off each mango with a knife before removing green skin with a standard kitchen peeler.

Combine all dressing ingredients — chilli sauce, sugar and light soy sauce — in a small mixing bowl.

Polygonum leaves are strong tasting, so be careful not to drown the flavours of the other ingredients in the dish when garnishing.

## Method

- In a large bowl, toss green mango shreds in combined dressing ingredients. Do not squeeze mango shreds or crispness will be lost. Adjust to taste with some sugar if mango is too sour.
- Transfer salad to a serving plate, then arrange cooked, peeled prawns on top.
- Garnish with chopped polygonum leaves and pounded peanuts.
- Serve salad with prawn crackers and dipping sauce.

Allow boiled pork thigh to cool completely before slicing. Otherwise, fat and skin may separate.

Juice from the halved water convolvulus stalks will emerge after kneading with salt for a few minutes.

After tossing, transfer water convolvulus stalks and desired amount of dressing to a serving plate or bowl.

*Step-By-Step*

# WATER CONVOLVULUS SALAD

Water convolvulus, or water spinach, is very rich in iron and is paired with a basic Vietnamese salad dressing here.

### Ingredients

| | |
|---|---|
| Water convolvulus | 1 kg (2 lb 3 oz), use stalks only |
| Salt | 2 Tbsp |
| Sesame seed oil | 2 tsp |
| Pork thigh | 200 g (7 oz), with a bit of skin and fat intact, boiled and thinly sliced |
| Prawns (shrimps) | 300 g (10½ oz), boiled and peeled but with tails intact |
| Polygonum (*laksa*) leaves | 20 g (¾ oz), stalks discarded and leaves coarsely chopped |
| Skinned peanuts (groundnuts) | 50 g (2 oz), roasted and coarsely pounded |
| Shallots | 30 g (1 oz), peeled, sliced and crisp-fried |

### Dressing

| | |
|---|---|
| Sugar | 6 Tbsp |
| Lime juice | 6 Tbsp |
| Chicken seasoning powder | 4 tsp |
| Fish sauce | 2 Tbsp |

### Dipping Sauce (combined)

| | |
|---|---|
| Fish sauce | 1 Tbsp |
| Coconut juice | 2 Tbsp, or boiled water |
| Sugar | 1 tsp |
| Vinegar | 1 Tbsp, or lemon juice |
| Garlic | 1 clove, peeled and minced |
| Red chilli (optional) | 1 or to taste, minced |

### Method

- Cut water convolvulus stalks into 8-cm (4-inch) lengths. Then, halve each length lengthways.
- Add salt to stalks and knead for a few minutes to extract the juice which tastes of tannins. Discard juice and rinse stalks well.
- Combine all dressing ingredients in a mixing bowl. Stir until sugar dissolves. Add stalks and toss together with sesame seed oil until well mixed.
- Transfer salad to a serving plate or bowl. Arrange pork slices and prawns on top.
- Garnish with chopped polygonum leaves, pounded peanuts and fried shallots. Serve with dipping sauce.

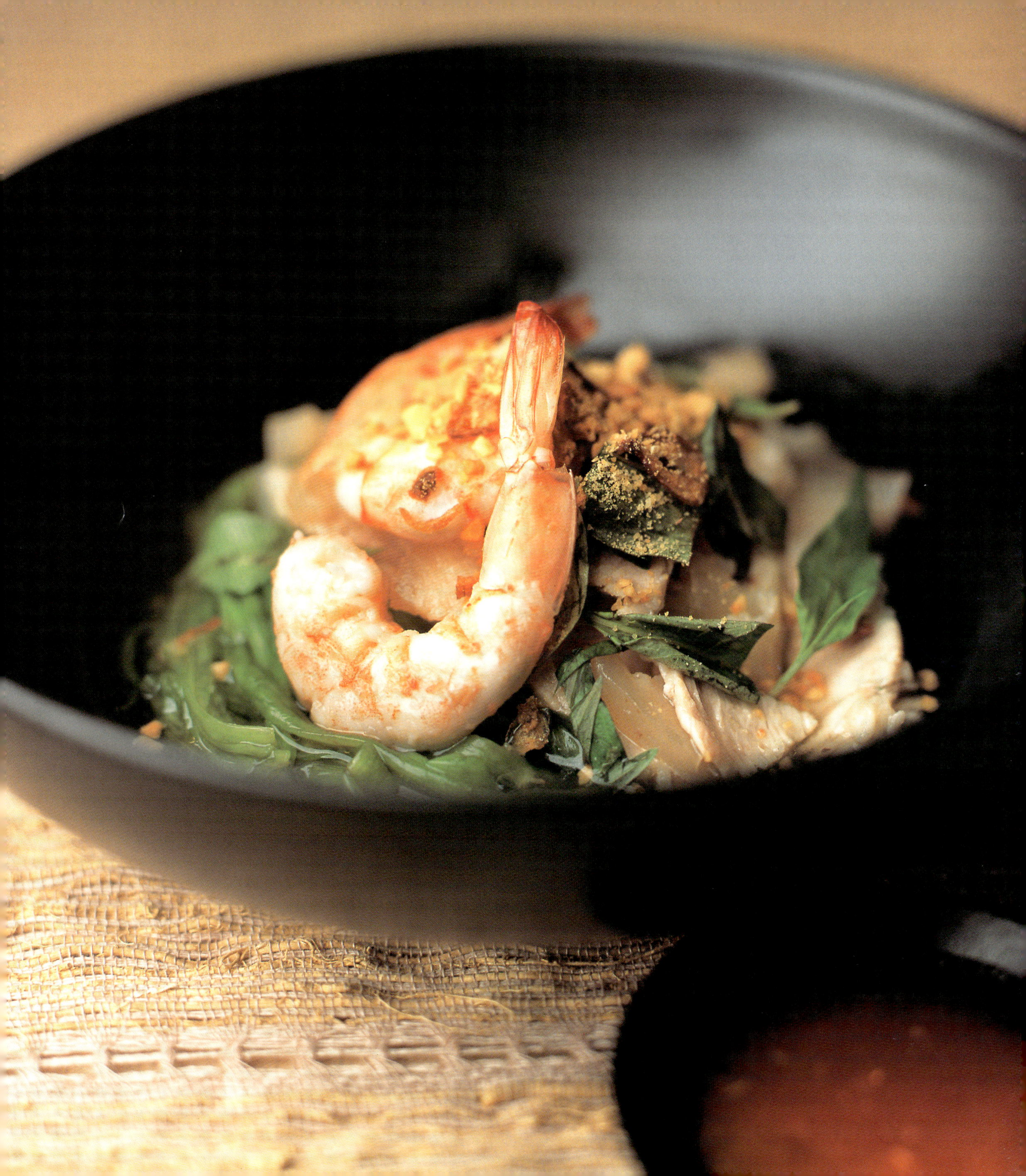

Raw prawn crackers are hard, dense discs and sink when lowered into hot oil. They fluff up and rise to the surface when cooked.

To make vinegar-water mixture, mix 3 parts water with 1 part vinegar. Soak sliced salad ingredients in the mixture to prevent discolouration.

Toss salad ingredients together until well mixed before transferring to a serving plate or bowl.

*Step-By-Step*

# BEEF SALAD

Star fruit slices make this salad refreshingly juicy, banana slices give it substance, while onion rings give bite and zing.

### Ingredients
| | |
|---|---|
| Beef fillet | 600 g (1 lb 5 oz) |
| Vinegar | as required |
| Water | as required |
| Unripe green banana | 1, peeled and thinly sliced |
| Unripe sour star fruits | 2, peeled and thinly sliced |
| Onions | 2, peeled and cut into thin rings |
| Cooking oil | 1–2 Tbsp |
| Coriander (cilantro) leaves | 20 g (3/4 oz), washed |
| Skinned peanuts (groundnuts) | 50 g (2 oz), roasted and coarsely pounded |
| Red chilli | 1, finely sliced |
| Shallots | 30 g (1 oz), peeled, sliced and crisp-fried |
| Prawn (shrimp) crackers | 20, deep-fried |

### Seasoning
| | |
|---|---|
| Chopped garlic | 2 tsp, pan-fried in oil until golden brown |
| Ground black pepper | 2 tsp |
| Sugar | 2 tsp |
| Sesame seed oil | 2 tsp |

### Method
- Slice beef thinly and across grain to ensure tenderness. Put beef slices into a bowl. Add seasoning ingredients and mix well. Set aside for 10 minutes.
- Make sufficient vinegar-water mixture (3 parts water to 1 part vinegar) to soak cut banana and star fruit slices, as well as onion rings separately.
- Heat oil in a skillet (frying pan) over high heat for 30 seconds. Add beef slices and stir-fry quickly, then remove from heat.
- Drain all soaked ingredients well. Then, combine with cooked beef in a mixing bowl and toss.
- Transfer tossed ingredients to a serving plate or bowl. Garnish as desired with coriander leaves, pounded peanuts, red chilli slices and fried shallots.
- Serve with prawn crackers and dipping sauce (see pg 38).

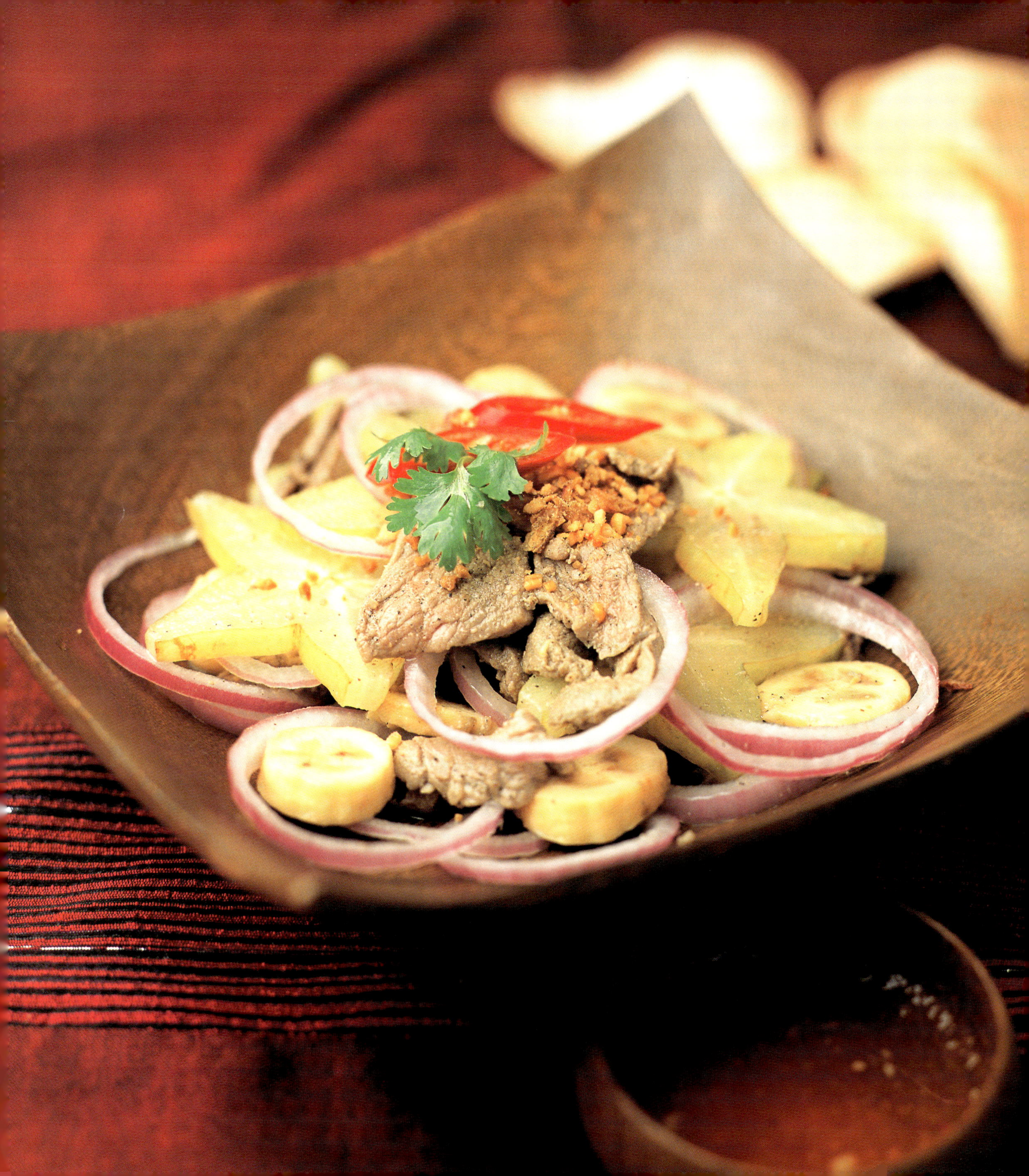

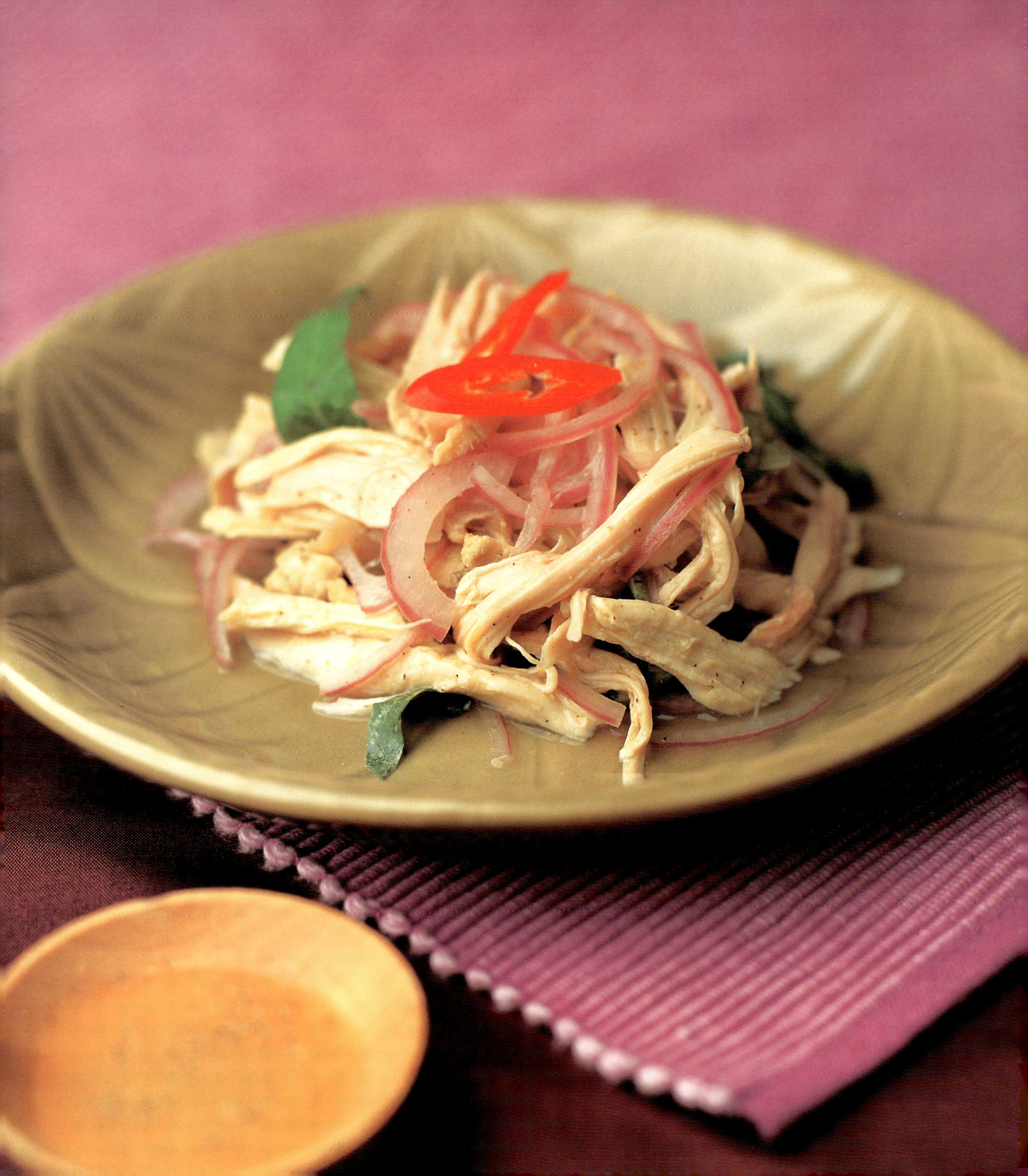

# CHICKEN SALAD WITH POLYGONUM LEAVES

A tangy and peppery salad of tender chicken, aromatic polygonum leaves and crisp onion strips will whet any sluggish appetite.

### Ingredients
| | |
|---|---|
| Vinegar | as required |
| Water | as required |
| Onions | 2, peeled and cut into half-moon slices |
| Chicken | 1, whole, 1.5–2 kg (3 lb 4½ oz–4 lb 6 oz) |
| Rice wine or vodka | 30 ml (1 fl oz) |
| Polygonum (*laksa*) leaves | 50 g (2 oz), washed and stalks discarded |
| Red chillies | 1–2, sliced |

### Seasoning
| | |
|---|---|
| Ground black pepper | 1 tsp |
| Chicken seasoning powder | 3 tsp |
| Sugar | 1½ Tbsp |
| Salt | 2 tsp |
| Lime juice | 3 Tbsp |

### Dipping Sauce (combined)
| | |
|---|---|
| Lime juice | 1 Tbsp |
| Salt | 2 tsp |
| Ground black pepper | 1 tsp |

## Step-By-Step

To cut half-moon slices, first halve onion lengthways. Then, with flat side down, slice across.

Instead of deboning cooked chicken, one could just tear meat off the bones and shred by hand.

After onion slices, add seasoning ingredients into bowl and mix well. Adjust to taste with more seasoning if necessary.

### Method

- Make sufficient vinegar-water mixture to soak onion slices. To make water-vinegar mixture, mix 3 parts water with 1 part vinegar. Drain onion slices well before use.
- Steam chicken for 20 minutes or until cooked through. Remove chicken from steamer and sprinkle rice wine or vodka all over. Return chicken to steamer and replace lid. Leave for 5 minutes, then remove from heat.
- Debone slightly cooled chicken and cut flesh into desired bite-sized pieces. Alternatively, shred chicken meat by hand.
- Put chicken pieces into a mixing bowl. Add polygonum leaves, drained onion slices and seasoning ingredients and mix.
- Transfer salad to a serving plate or bowl. Add chilli slices on top.
- Serve with dipping sauce.

Fish and Pineapple Stew

Baked Crabs

Steamed Fish with Sugar Cane

Steamed Fish with Fermented Soy Beans

Stir-fried Minced Eel with Lemon Grass

Fried Crab in Tamarind Sauce

Prawns Sautéed with Pork Belly

Stuffed Squid

SEAFOOD

Use only a sharp knife or cleaver to cut pineapple into thin slices. A blunt knife will split the fibres and cause broken slices.

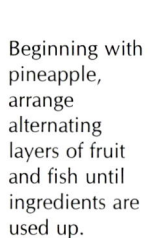

Beginning with pineapple, arrange alternating layers of fruit and fish until ingredients are used up.

If liquid level does not surpass ingredients, top up with more coconut juice or water.

*Step-By-Step*

# FISH AND PINEAPPLE STEW

Tangy pineapple slices tame the pungent taste of fish sauce in this dish, while the bird's eye chillies impart fiery spiciness.

### Ingredients

| | |
|---|---|
| Tuna | 1 kg (2 lb 3 oz), cut into 1-cm (1/2-inch) thick pieces |
| Minced garlic | 2 tsp |
| Chicken seasoning powder | 3 tsp |
| Ground black pepper | 1 tsp |
| Cooking oil | 5 Tbsp |
| Pineapple | 1, peeled, quartered lengthways, cored and cut into 0.5-cm (1/4-inch) thick slices |
| Bird's eye chillies | 5, halved |
| Fish sauce | 50 ml (1 3/4 fl oz) or more to taste |
| Coconut juice | 500 ml (16 fl oz / 2 cups) |
| Spring onions (scallions) | 5, peeled and cut into 5-cm (2-inch) lengths |

### Method

- Season fish with garlic, seasoning powder and pepper. Set aside for 30 minutes to 1 hour.
- Heat oil in a skillet (frying pan). Add seasoned fish and cook until golden brown. Dish out and set aside.
- Use a clay or heavy-based pot to stew. Arrange a layer of pineapple pieces to cover base of vessel, followed by a layer of fish on top. Arrange a second layer of pineapple atop fish, followed by a second layer of fish.
- Arrange alternating layers until the 2 ingredients are used up. Chillies will be placed last and right on top.
- Pour in fish sauce and coconut juice to cover ingredients. Simmer over low heat for 30 minutes or until liquid thickens.
- Garnish as desired with spring onions before serving.

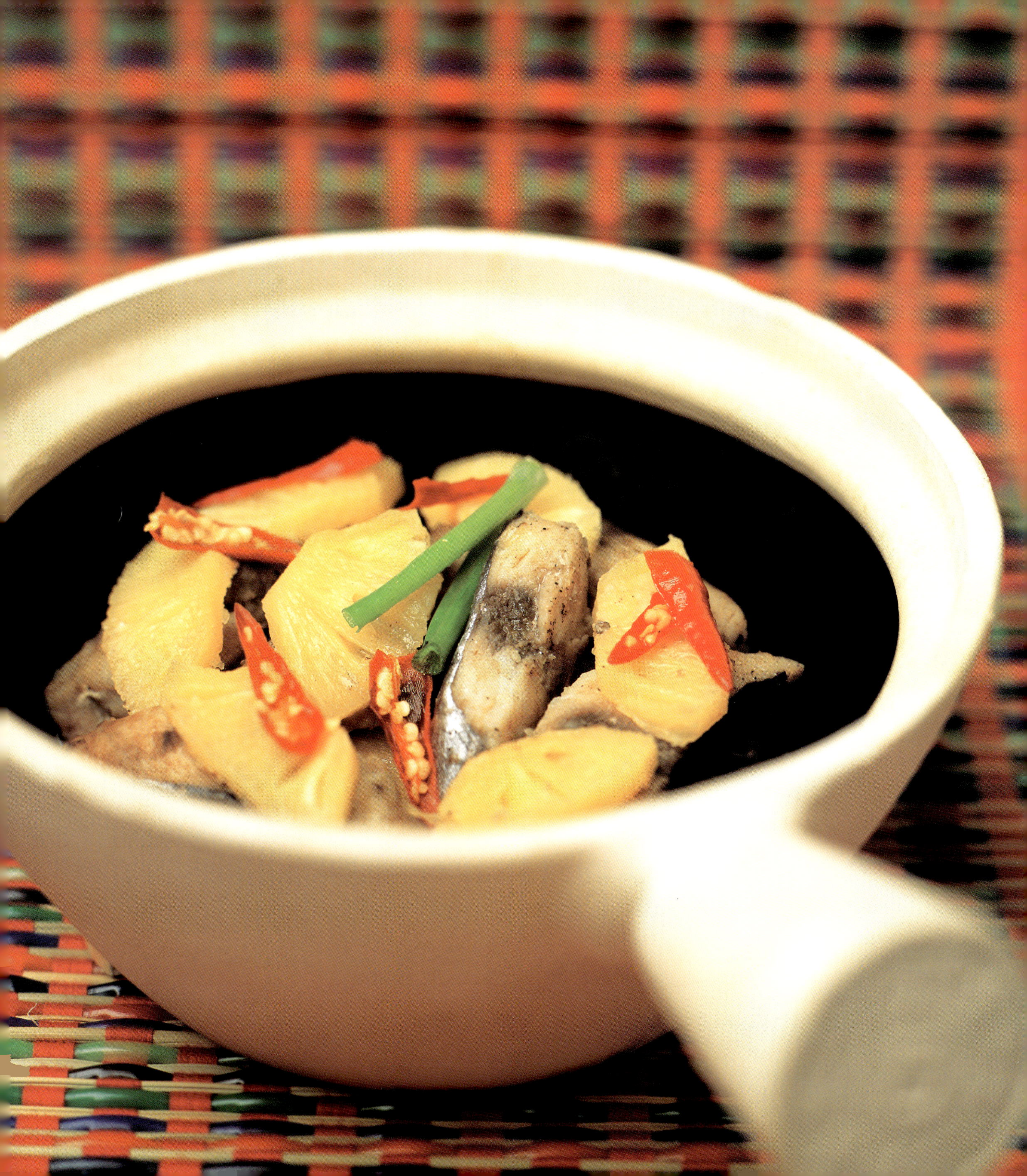

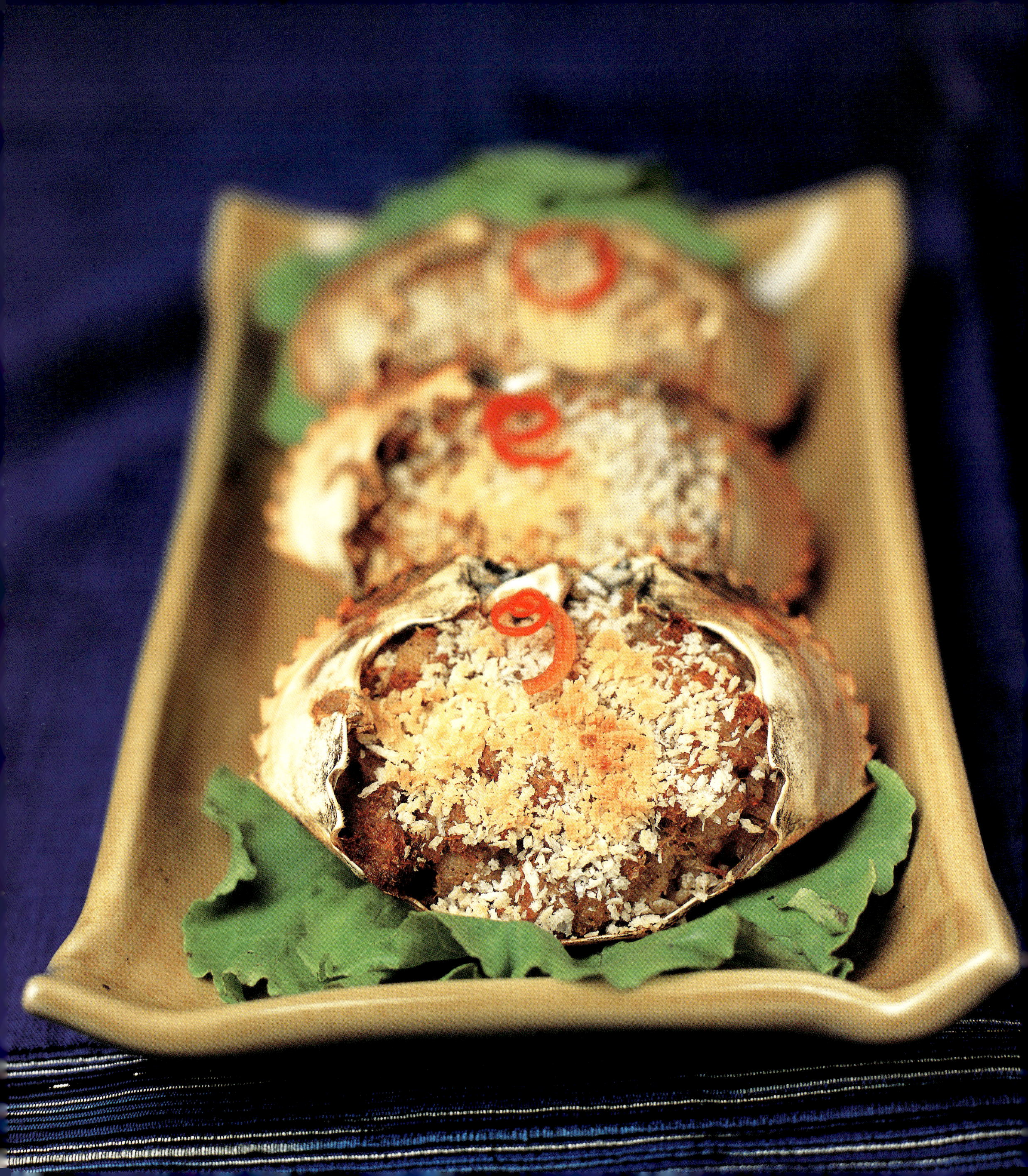

# BAKED CRABS

Crab top shells filled with juicy, creamy crabmeat and sealed with golden bread crumb crusts make a great meal and talking point.

### Ingredients

| | |
|---|---|
| Fresh milk | 250 ml (8 fl oz / 1 cup) |
| Bread | 2 slices, crusts discarded and torn into small pieces |
| Butter | 50 g (2 oz) |
| Minced garlic | 1 tsp |
| Minced shallot | 1 tsp |
| Crabs | 3, about 1 kg (2 lb 3 oz), washed, steamed until cooked, top shells and grey crab curd on underside reserved and meat extracted |
| Crispy breadcrumbs | 20 g (3/4 oz) |
| Red chilli shreds (optional) | for garnishing |
| Chinese lettuce leaves (optional) | for garnishing |

### Seasoning

| | |
|---|---|
| Ground black pepper | 1/4 tsp |
| Salt | 1 tsp |
| Chicken seasoning powder | 1 tsp |

### Step-By-Step

Steam cleaned crabs over rapidly boiling water to cook.

Use either a fine strainer or muslin cloth to squeeze out half the milk in the milk-soaked bread.

When stuffing the top shells, use the back of a spoon to press down on the filling and pack firmly.

### Method

- Combine milk and bread in a bowl. Leave to soak for 15 minutes or until bread is soft and soggy. Then, squeeze out about half the milk. A soft, smooth paste should result.
- Heat butter in a wok or skillet (frying pan). Add garlic and shallot and fry until fragrant. Add crab curd and -meat and fry for 5–10 minutes before removing from heat.
- Mix cooked crabmeat and milk-soaked bread together, then add seasoning ingredients. Adjust to taste if necessary.
- Stuff each top shell with crabmeat mixture, then sprinkle on breadcrumbs to cover surface.
- Bake in an oven preheated to 350°C/662°F for about 5 minutes or until surface is golden brown.
- Serve garnished on a bed of lettuce leaves with chilli shreds.

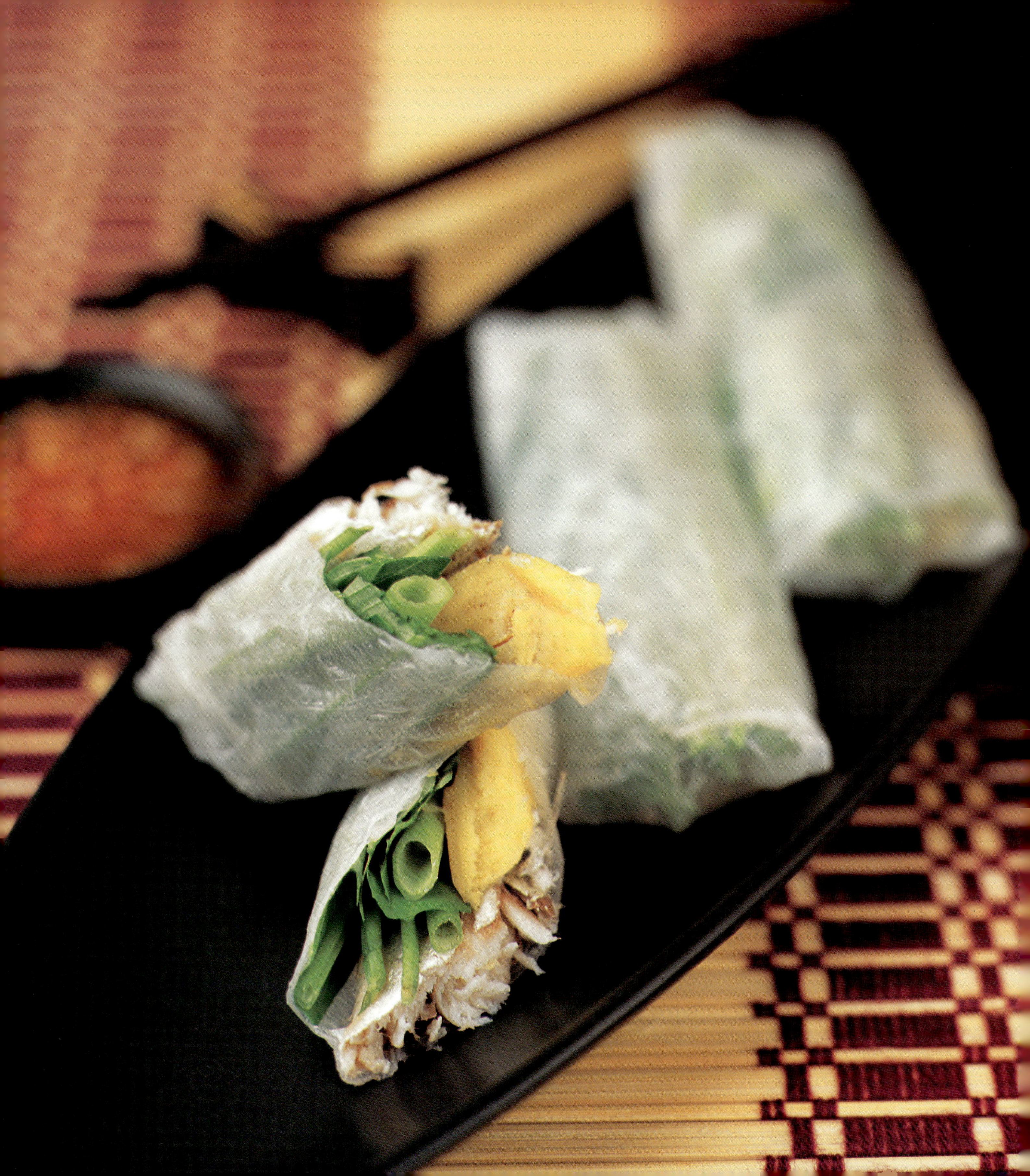

# STEAMED FISH WITH SUGAR CANE

With all the natural juices sealed in during stewing, the fish meat here is succulent and brushed with sugar cane sweetness.

### Ingredients

| | |
|---|---|
| Sugar cane | 5 sticks, each 10 cm (4 inches), washed, peeled and quartered lengthways |
| Sardines | 1 kg (2 lb 3 oz), 9–10 fishes, washed in salted water and drained well, or 1 kg chubb mackerel |
| Water | 500 ml (16 fl oz / 2 cups) |
| Round rice papers | 10 sheets, 20 cm (8 inches) in diameter |
| Sweet potato | 1, steamed, peeled and sliced into 6 pieces lengthways |
| Water convolvulus | 1 kg (2 lb 3 oz), roots discarded, washed and cut into 10-cm (4-inch) sections |

### Dipping Sauce (combined)

| | |
|---|---|
| Fish sauce | 1 Tbsp |
| Coconut juice | 2 Tbsp, or boiled water |
| Sugar | 1 tsp |
| Vinegar | 1 Tbsp, or lemon juice |
| Garlic | 1 clove, peeled and minced |
| Red chilli (optional) | 1 or to taste, minced |

## Step-By-Step

A cleaver is the ideal cutting tool for peeling tough and fibrous sugar cane.

At the end of cooking time, remove only the cooked fish. Discard sugar cane and stewing liquid.

Assemble the rolls to serve or allow diners to assemble their own rolls at the table.

### Method

- Line bottom of a pot with a layer of sugar cane strips, followed by a layer of sardines on top. Arrange a second layer of sugar cane strips atop fish, followed by a second layer of fish.
- Continue to arrange alternating layers of sugar cane and fish until both ingredients are used up.
- Pour water into pot and cook over high heat for 20 minutes.
- Turn off heat and transfer fish to a serving plate, along with sweet potato slices and water convolvulus.
- To assemble, place a sheet of rice paper on a plate. Smear on water to soften, then put half a sardine, a sweet potato slice and some water convolvulus on top. Fold lower edge over ingredients, then fold in left and right sides and roll up firmly.
- Eat rolls with dipping sauce.

Squeeze ready soaked black fungus of excess water before cutting into shreds.

For diamond shapes, make parallel 45° cuts, 5 cm (2 inches) apart, on each cabbage leaf. Then, halve each strip by cutting across diagonally.

Distribute the complementary ingredients as desired, whether under over or around fish.

*Step-By-Step*

# STEAMED FISH WITH FERMENTED SOY BEANS

Laden with complementary ingredients, the fish here is only half the show, and the soy bean paste is what holds all the flavours together.

### Ingredients

| | |
|---|---|
| Garoupa, red snapper or sea bass | 1, whole, about 1 kg (2 lb 3 oz) |
| Salt | 1 Tbsp |
| Cooking oil | as required |
| Transparent (glass) vermicelli | 10 g ($1/3$ oz), cut into 5-cm (2-inch) lengths then soaked in water to soften |
| Dried black (wood ear) fungus | 5 g ($1/6$ oz), soaked in water to soften then shredded |
| Chinese (napa) cabbage | 1 head, about 500 g (1 lb $1^1/2$ oz), cut into 5-cm (2-inch) wide diamond-shaped pieces |
| Tomatoes | 2, each cut into 6 wedges |
| Ginger (optional) | 1–2-cm ($1/2$–1-inch) knob, peeled and julienned |
| Onion | 1, peeled and cut into wedges |
| Preserved soy bean paste | 100 g ($3^1/2$ oz) |
| Red chilli | 1, sliced |
| Coriander (cilantro) leaves | for garnishing |

### Seasoning (combined)

| | |
|---|---|
| Light soy sauce | 1 tsp |
| Sugar | 1 tsp |
| Ground white pepper | 1 tsp |

### Method

- Clean and wash fish. Then, dry and rub all over with salt. Pan-fry with a little oil until slightly golden.
- Place fish onto a large serving plate. Evenly distribute all remaining ingredients over and around fish.
- Pour seasoning ingredients over fish.
- Steam until cooked, then garnish as desired and serve.

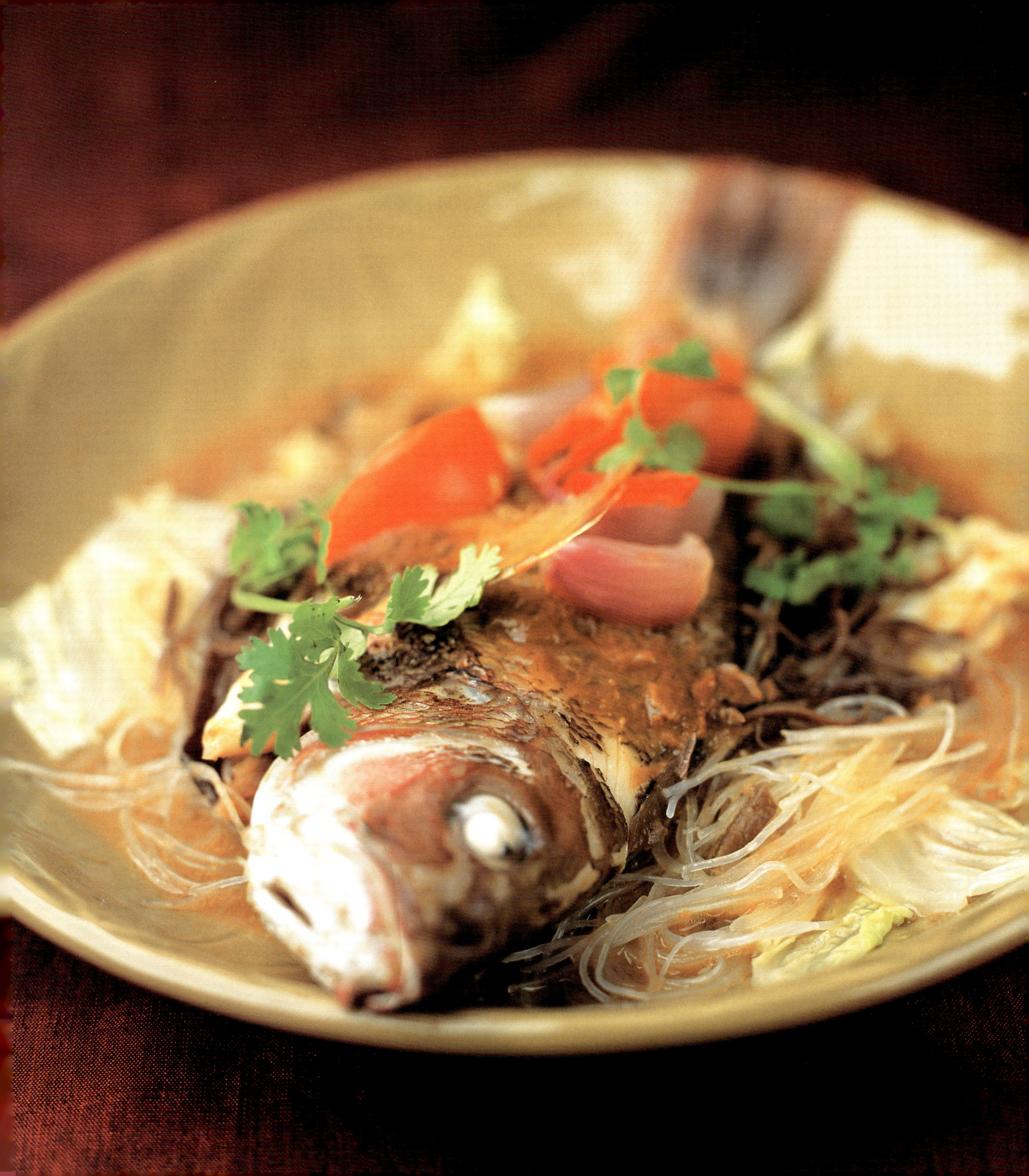

To debone an eel, first discard head and cut body into shorter lengths for easier handling. Then, fillet each length.

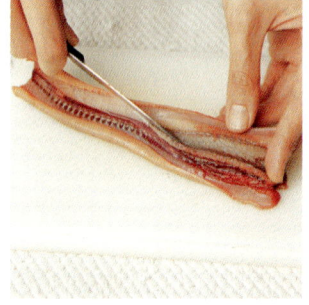

Either chop eel, lard, onions and garlic together until minced or combine in a blender (food processor).

Add in the mince only when the lemon grass and chillies have become golden and very fragrant.

*Step-By-Step*

# STIR-FRIED MINCED EEL WITH LEMON GRASS

The spicy and aromatic combination of onions, garlic, lemon grass and chillies remove any hint of fishiness from this dish.

### Ingredients
| | |
|---|---|
| Eel | 2, washed and deboned |
| Lard | 50 g (2 oz) |
| Onions | 50 g (2 oz), peeled and minced |
| Garlic | 50 g (2 oz), peeled and minced |
| Cooking oil | 125 ml (4 fl oz / ½ cup) |
| Minced lemon grass | 3 tsp |
| Minced red chillies | 3 tsp |
| Fish sauce | 1 tsp |
| Chinese lettuce leaves (optional) | for garnishing |
| Skinned peanuts (groundnuts) | 50 g (2 oz), roasted and coarsely pounded |
| Sesame crackers | 20, 30 x 30 cm (12 x 12 inches), deep-fried, replaceable with papadums or prawn crackers |

### Seasoning
| | |
|---|---|
| Salt | ½ tsp |
| Sugar | ½ tsp |
| Chicken seasoning powder | ½ tsp |

### Method

- Chop eel, lard, onions and garlic together until minced. Mix in seasoning ingredients.
- Heat oil in a cooking pan or wok. Fry lemon grass and chilli until golden brown.
- Add chopped eel mixture and stir-fry until cooked. Season with fish sauce, then dish out.
- Serve garnished with lettuce, if desired. Add roasted peanuts on top.
- To eat, use crackers to scoop cooked ingredients.

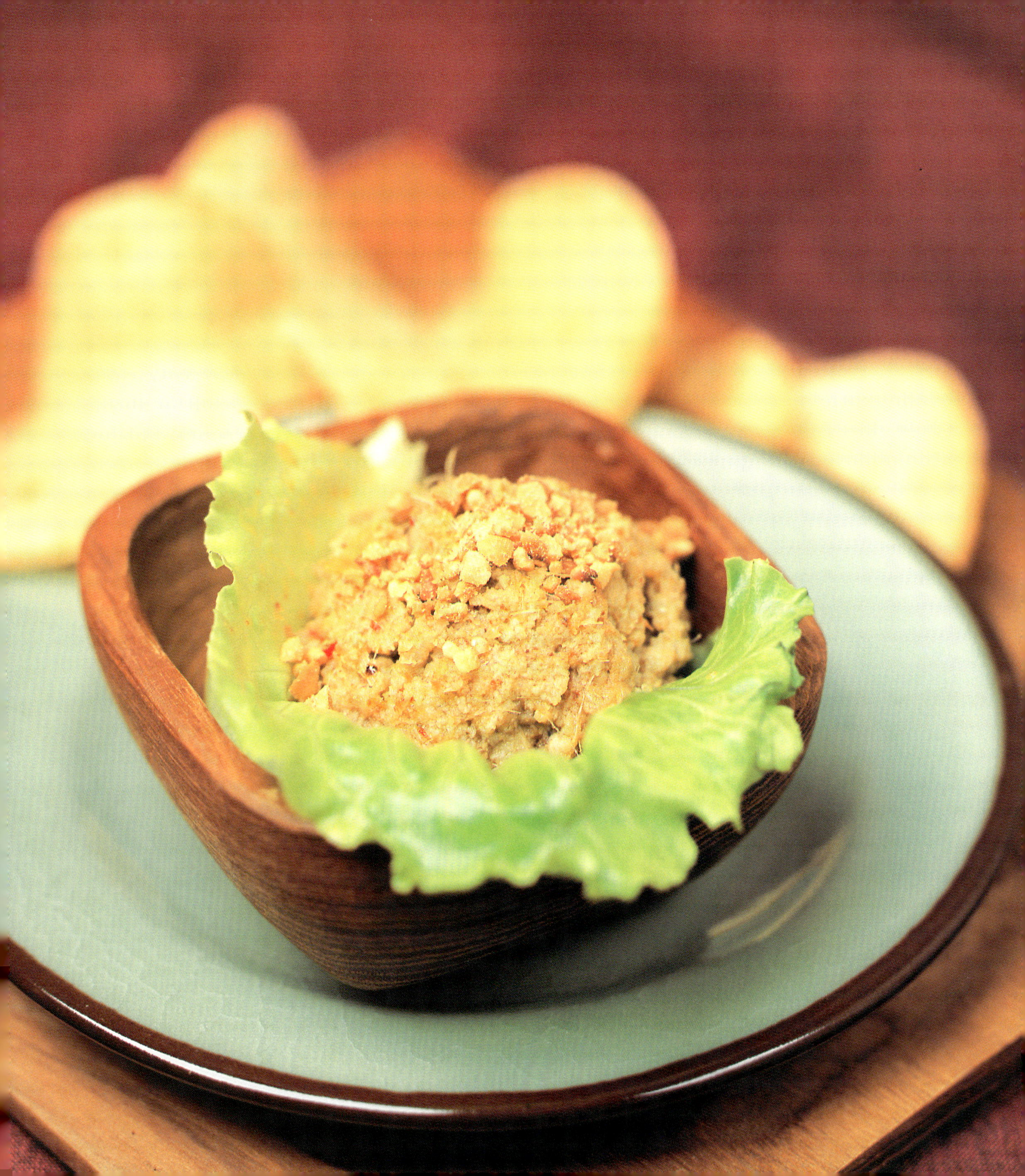

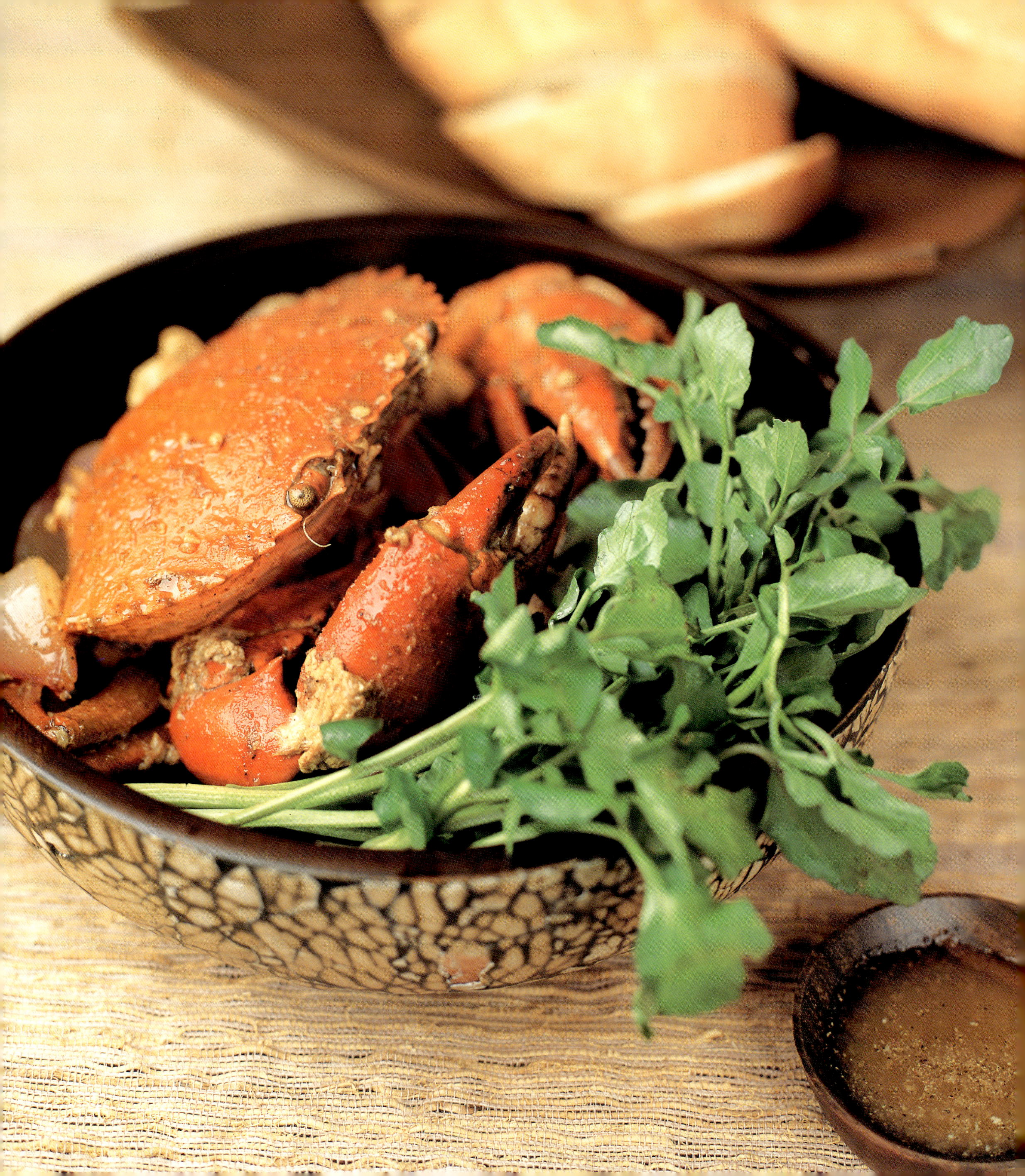

# FRIED CRAB IN TAMARIND SAUCE

A quaint rendition of the sweet-and-sour formula, this crab dish has a delightfully balanced and appetising flavour.

### Ingredients

| | |
|---|---|
| Cooking oil | 500 ml (16 fl oz / 2 cups) |
| Crab(s) | 1–2, about 1 kg (2 lb 3 oz), washed, top shell(s) and grey crab curd underside reserved, pincers separated and cracked and remaining crab(s) quartered |
| Onion | 1, peeled and cut into wedges |
| Minced garlic | 2 tsp |
| Minced shallots | 2 tsp |
| Tamarind pulp | 50 g (2 oz), soaked in root beer or sarsaparilla (sarsi) |
| Root beer or sarsaparilla | 250 ml (8 fl oz / 1 cup) |
| Watercress | 100 g (3½ oz) |
| French loaf | 1 |

### Seasoning

| | |
|---|---|
| Salt | ¼ tsp |
| Ground black pepper | ¼ tsp |
| Sugar | ¼ tsp |
| Chicken seasoning powder | ¼ tsp or to taste |

### Dipping Sauce (combined)

| | |
|---|---|
| Lime juice | 1 Tbsp |
| Salt | 2 tsp |
| Ground black pepper | 1 tsp |

## Step-By-Step

Add enough root beer or sarsaparilla to cover tamarind pulp, then stir and set aside.

Locate a triangular flap near crab's hind legs, on the underside. Insert the tip of a small knife there and pry top shell loose.

After dishing out, arrange crab pieces neatly and place top shell(s) on top for better presentation.

### Method

- Heat oil in a wok. Add crab pincers and fry for 4 minutes, then add crab quarters and cook for 5 minutes. Lastly, add top shell(s) and cook for 3 minutes. Drain and set aside.
- Remove the bulk of oil, leaving about 4 Tbsp in wok. Add onion wedges and stir-fry briefly, then dish out and set aside.
- In the same oil, stir-fry garlic and shallots until fragrant. Add tamarind, root beer and fried onion wedges. Cook over medium heat until liquid reaches the boil.
- Add crab pieces and cover with lid to cook. Stir occasionally.
- When liquid is thickened, add crab curd and mix well. Then, add seasoning ingredients. Adjust to taste if necessary before removing from heat.
- Transfer to a serving plate or bowl with watercress on the side.
- Eat with French loaf slices and dipping sauce.

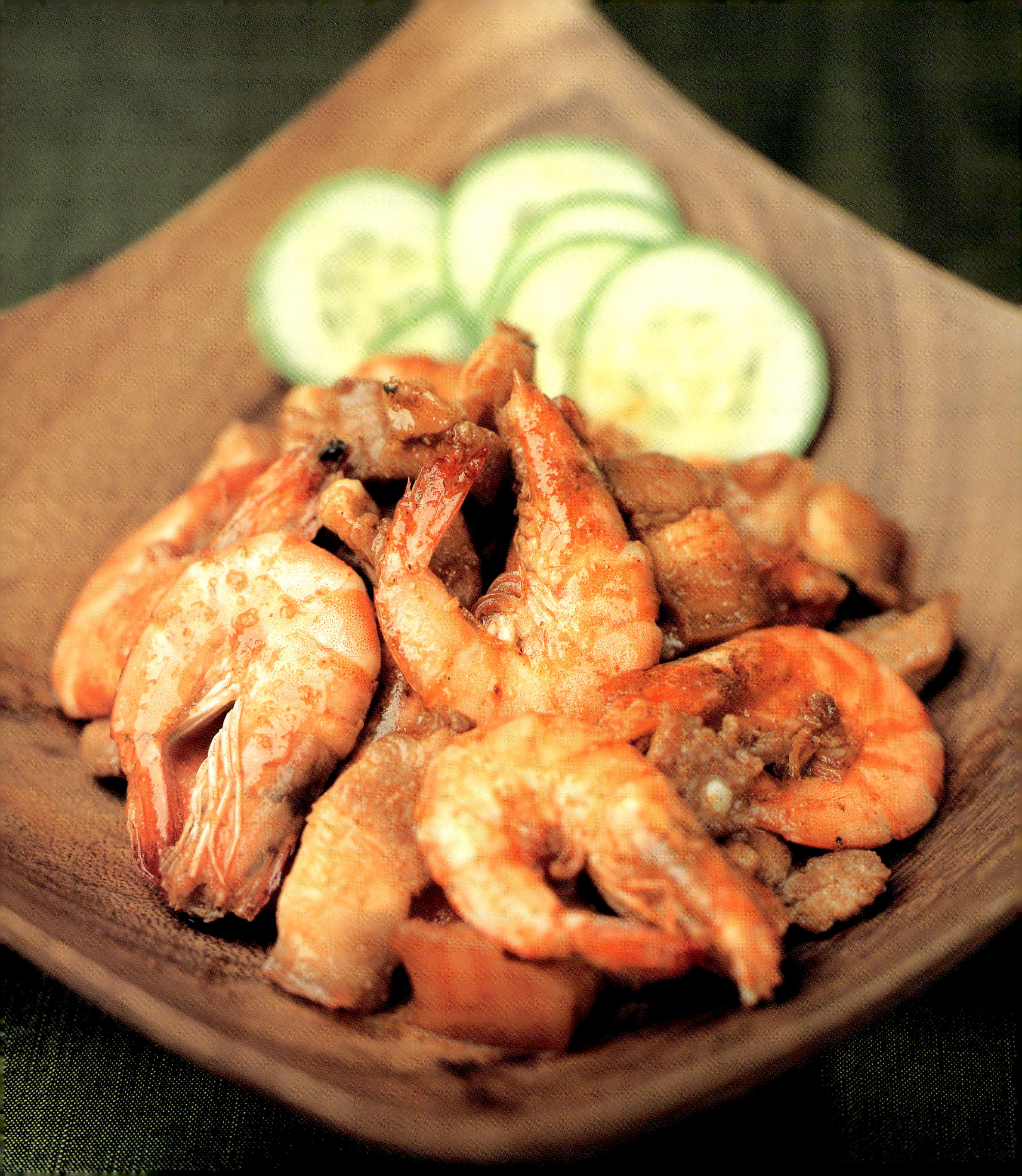

# PRAWNS SAUTÉED WITH PORK BELLY

Plain steamed rice best brings out the tastes and textures of this richly flavourful dish.

### Ingredients

| | |
|---|---|
| Freshwater prawns (shrimps) | 300 g (10½ oz), washed and trimmed of feelers and sharp tips of heads |
| Pork belly | 300 g (10½ oz), washed and sliced |
| Salt | 1 tsp |
| Chicken seasoning powder | 2 tsp |
| Cooking oil | 1 Tbsp |
| Minced garlic | 1 tsp |
| Cucumber | 1, peeled if desired, washed and sliced |

### Seasoning Ingredients

| | |
|---|---|
| Sugar | 1 tsp |
| Fish sauce | 1 Tbsp |
| Chilli powder | 1 tsp |

**Step-By-Step**

Using a pair of kitchen scissors, trim off feelers and sharp tips of prawn heads.

Cut cleaned pork belly into similarly sized pieces so that they will cook evenly later.

After adding seasoning ingredients, sauté prawns until liquid is nearly dried up before dishing out.

### Method

- Season prawns and pork slices with salt and seasoning powder.
- Heat cooking oil in a wok. Add garlic and stir-fry until fragrant.
- Add prawns and pork pieces and sauté for 5 minutes or until just cooked. Then, add seasoning ingredients and sauté for a few minutes more.
- When liquid is much reduced, remove from heat and transfer to a serving plate.
- Serve with cucumber slices on the side.

## Step-By-Step

To devein a prawn without cutting it open, use a toothpick or cocktail stick to dig out a bit of it, then pull gently.

Fill squid tubes with stuffing until firm, then sew openings together with a needle and thread.

Coat stuffed squid tubes well with beaten egg before rolling in flour so that flour will stick, making for a crispy outer layer later.

# STUFFED SQUID

A versatile dish, the deep-fried stuffed squids here can be one of several dishes served at mealtimes, a starter or a tasty afternoon snack.

### Ingredients

| | |
|---|---|
| Pork | 100 g (3½ oz) |
| Prawns (shrimps) | 200 g (7 oz), washed, peeled and deveined |
| Minced onion | 1 tsp |
| Minced garlic | 1 tsp |
| Salt | 1 tsp |
| Chicken seasoning powder | 2 tsp |
| Squids | 500 g (1 lb 1½ oz), heads separated, hard strips discarded, bodies thoroughly washed and skinned |
| Cooking oil | 2 Tbsp + enough for deep-frying |
| Minced shallot | 1 tsp |
| Tomato sauce (ketchup) | 3 Tbsp |
| Ground black pepper | 1 tsp |
| Sugar | ½ tsp |
| Egg | 1 |
| Plain (all-purpose) flour | 100 g (3½ oz) |
| Iceberg or Chinese lettuce | about 20 leaves, separated and washed |
| Chilli sauce | as required |

### Method

- Cut pork and peeled prawns into smaller pieces. Then, blend (process) them together with onion and garlic until pasty. Transfer paste to a bowl.
- Season paste with ½ tsp salt and 1 tsp seasoning powder. Then, stuff into squid bodies. Sew up open ends to secure.
- Heat oil in a wok. Fry shallot until fragrant. Add tomato sauce and stir well. Remove sauce and season with remaining salt and seasoning powder, as well as pepper and sugar.
- Beat egg well. Dip squids in, then coat with flour.
- Heat sufficient oil in a clean wok for deep-frying, then cook coated, stuffed squids until done.
- Arrange lettuce and cooked squids on serving plate, then pour on prepared sauce.
- Serve with chilli sauce.

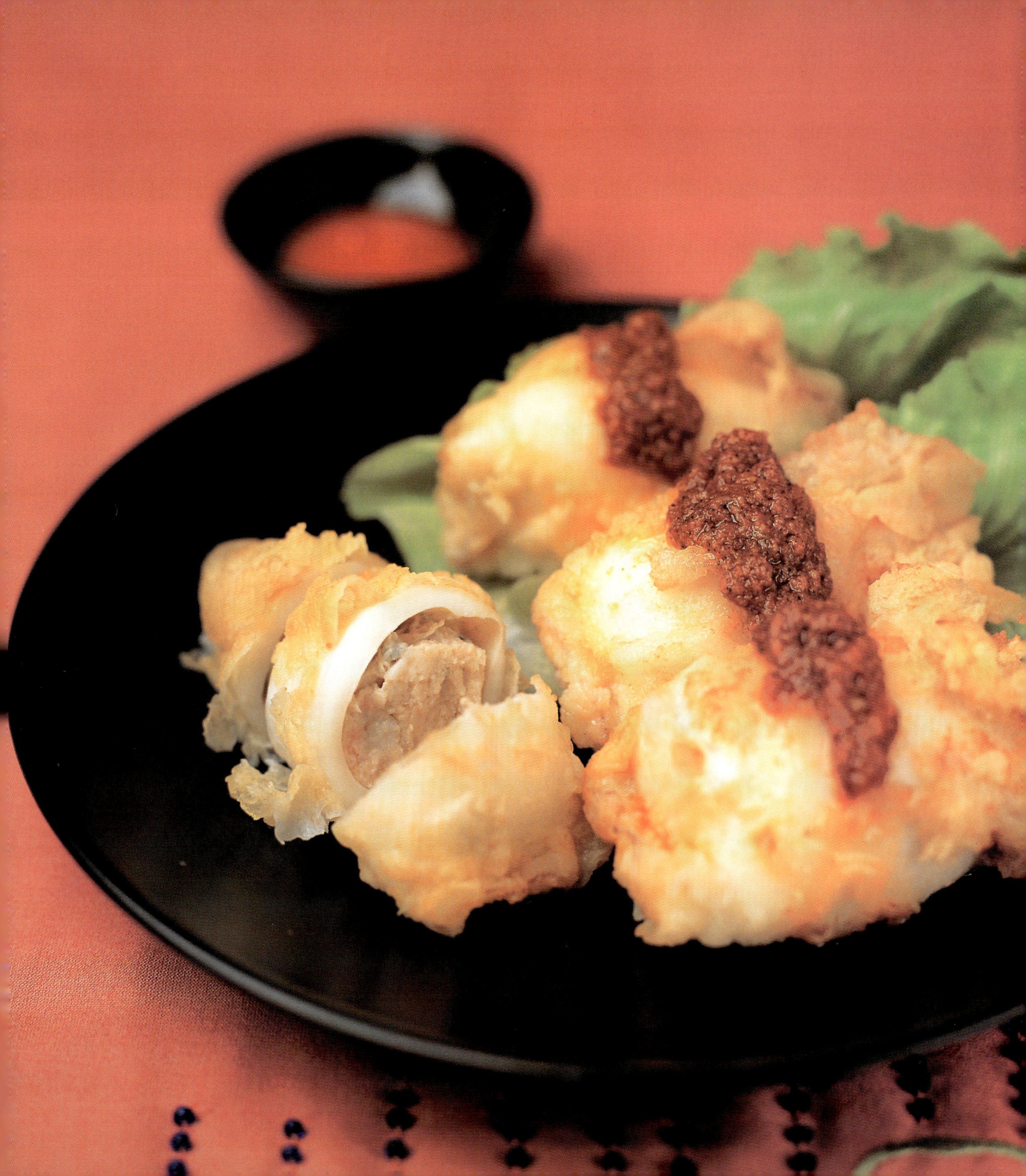

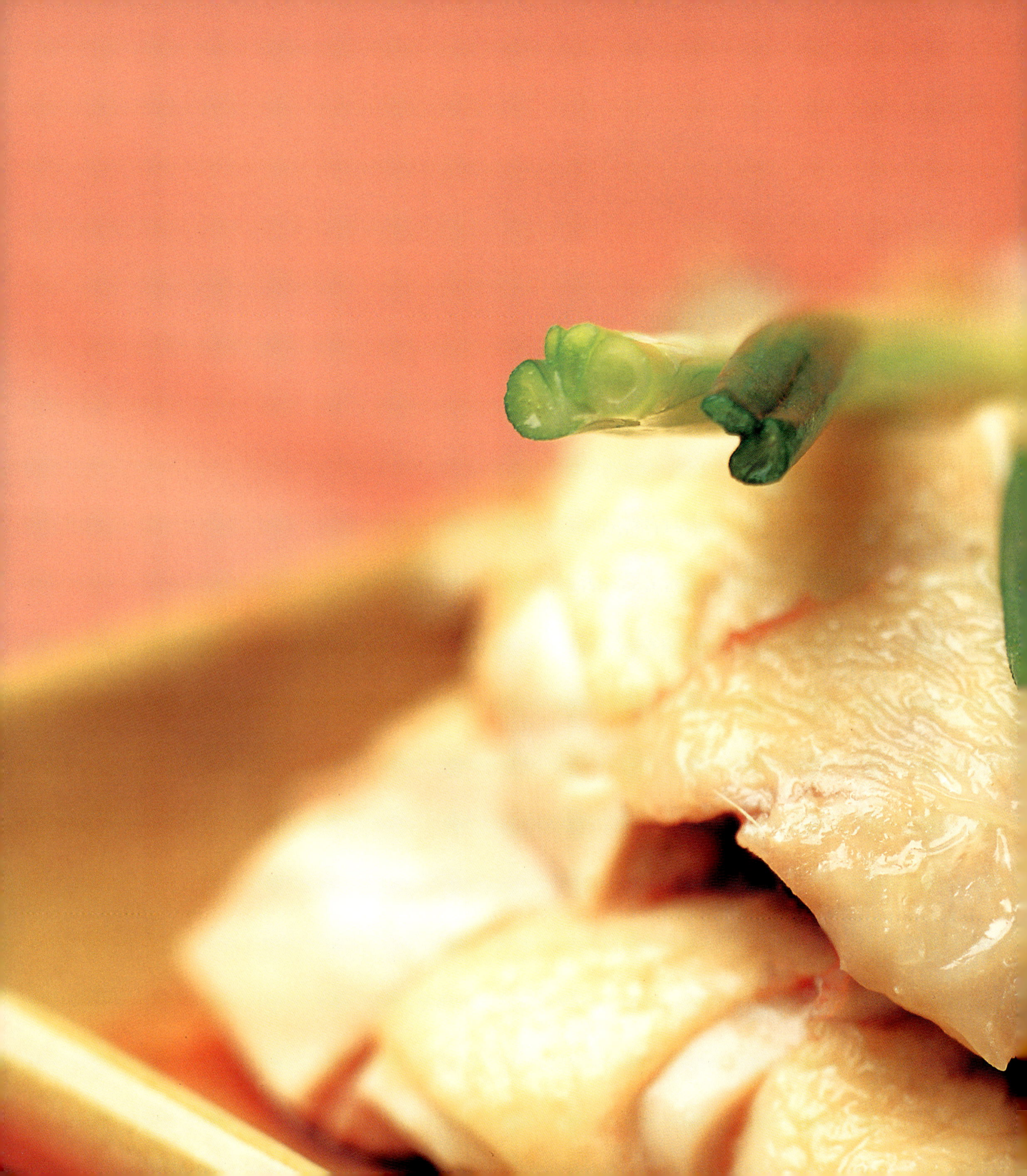

Fried Lemon Grass Chicken
Steamed Chicken with Spring Onions
Vietnamese Beef Stew
Beef on Fire
Beef Cooked in Vinegar
Steamed Minced Pork with Duck Eggs
Pork Stewed in Coconut Juice
Stir-fried Frog in Coconut Milk

# MEAT & POULTRY

Using a meat cleaver, cut chicken into smaller, bite-sized pieces.

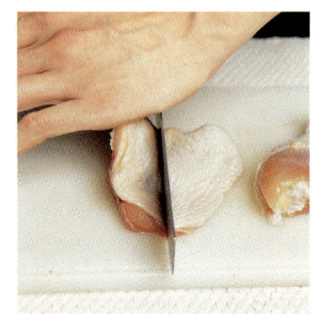

Slice bruised lemon grass stalks across for small rounds to put into a blender (food processor) to mince.

In a bowl, stir chicken pieces and marinade until well mixed.

*Step-By-Step*

# FRIED LEMON GRASS CHICKEN

Chicken pieces are dyed bright yellow by turmeric and flavoured by aromatic lemon grass and garlic.

### Ingredients

| | |
|---|---|
| Chicken pieces | 1 kg (2 lb 3 oz), washed and cut into bite-sized pieces |
| Cooking oil | 125 ml (4 fl oz / $1/2$ cup) |
| Minced garlic | 1 tsp |
| Coriander (cilantro) leaves (optional) | for garnishing |

### Marinade (combined)

| | |
|---|---|
| Minced lemon grass | 3 Tbsp, use hard stalk parts only and bruise to release fragrance before mincing |
| Chicken seasoning powder | 3 tsp |
| Turmeric powder | $1/2$ tsp |
| Minced red chilli | 1 tsp |
| Salt | 2 tsp |

### Method

- Marinate chicken pieces for 30 minutes to 1 hour.
- Heat oil in a skillet (frying pan) until hot, then add garlic and fry until fragrant.
- Add marinated chicken and cook until golden brown.
- Garnish if desired and serve.

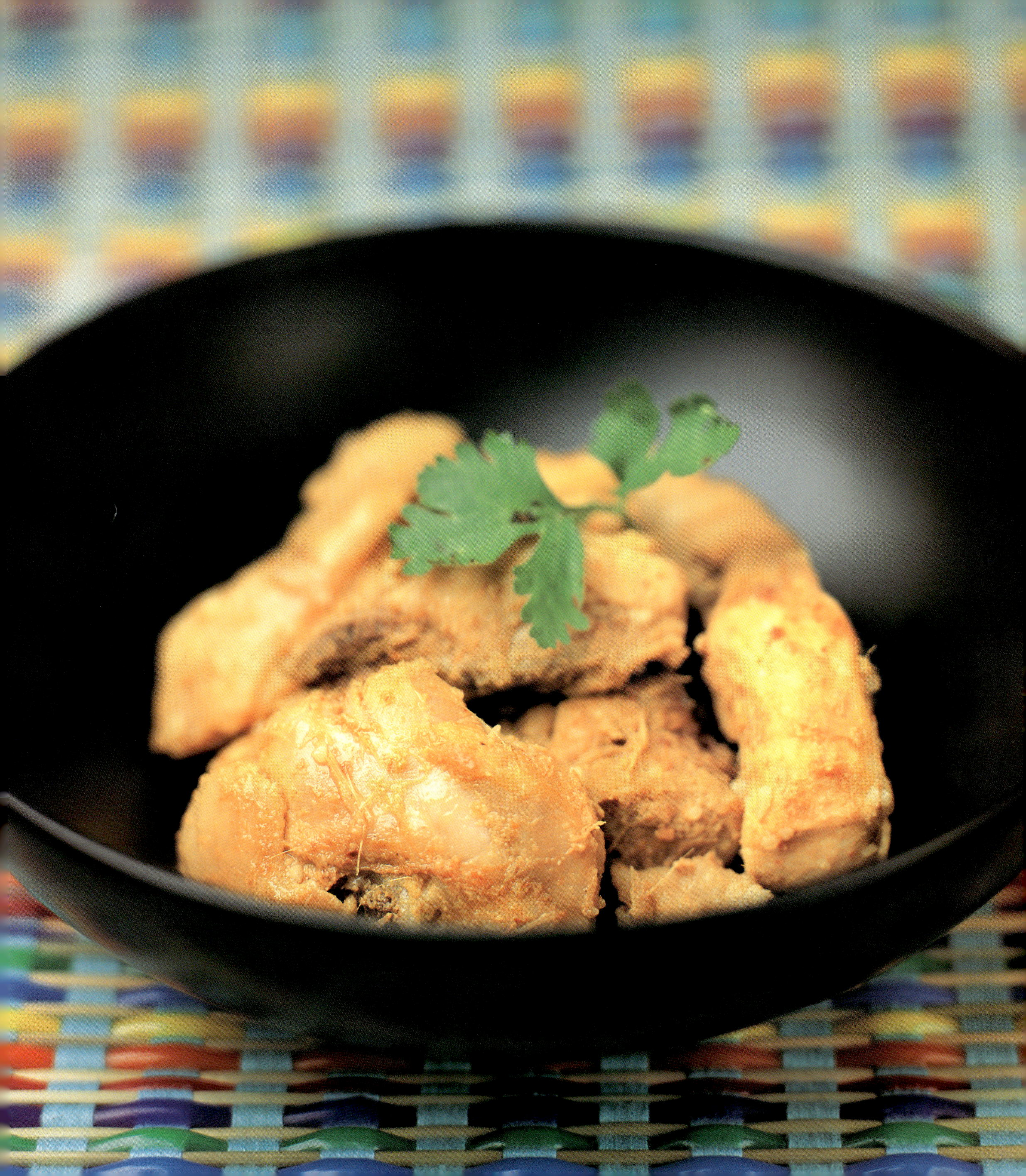

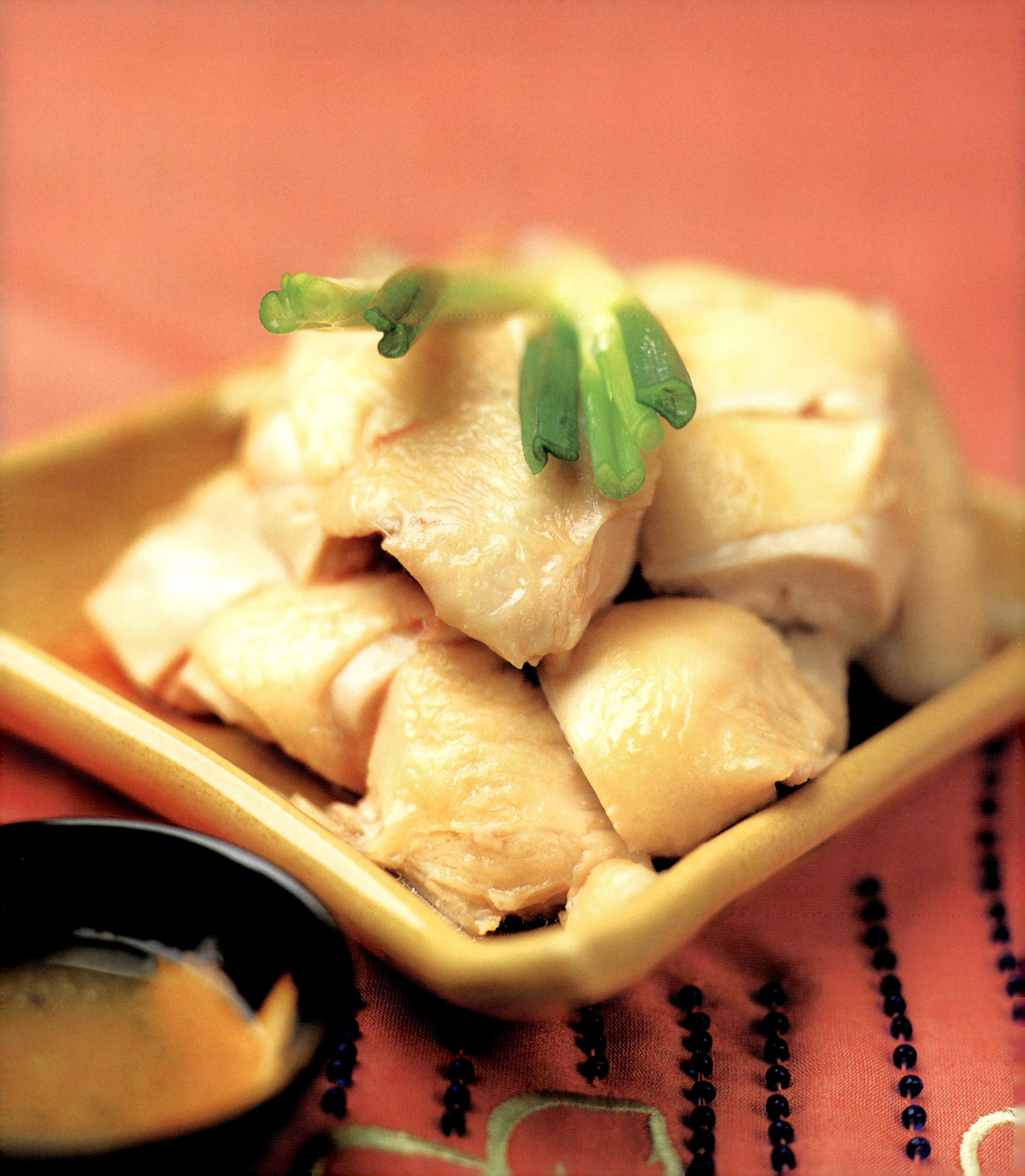

# STEAMED CHICKEN WITH SPRING ONIONS

The natural flavours of the chicken are enhanced ever so subtly and yet so indispensably by ginger, sesame seed oil and spring onions.

### Ingredients
| | |
|---|---|
| Chicken | 1, whole, about 2 kg (4 lb 6 oz) |
| Ginger | 10 g (1/3 oz), peeled and finely shredded |
| Chicken seasoning powder | 3 tsp |
| Salt | 2 tsp |
| Sesame seed oil | 2 tsp |
| Spring onions (scallions) | 300 g (10 1/2 oz), peeled and cut into 15-cm (6-inch) lengths, use hard stalk parts only |

### Dipping Sauce (combined)
| | |
|---|---|
| Lime juice | 1 Tbsp |
| Salt | 2 tsp |
| Ground black pepper | 1 tsp |

**Step-By-Step**

Peel ginger by scraping with the knife's cutting edge. Slice peeled knob thinly, then lay slices flat and cut into shreds.

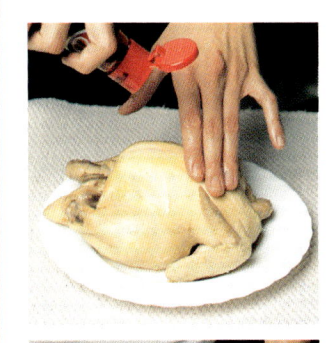

Rubbing sesame seed oil onto the skin of cooked chicken skin imparts fragrance and prevents drying out.

Blanch spring onion stalks to cook slightly and for a deeper, richer green colour.

### Method
- Season chicken with ginger, seasoning powder and salt. Set aside for about 1 hour.
- Steam chicken for about 40 minutes or until cooked. Smear sesame seed oil onto skin of cooked chicken.
- Blanch spring onions for about 1 minute, then drain and set aside.
- Chop chicken into bite-sized pieces and arrange neatly on a serving plate. Place spring onion lengths on top. Alternatively, divide chicken pieces into desired serving portions and garnish.
- Serve with dipping sauce.

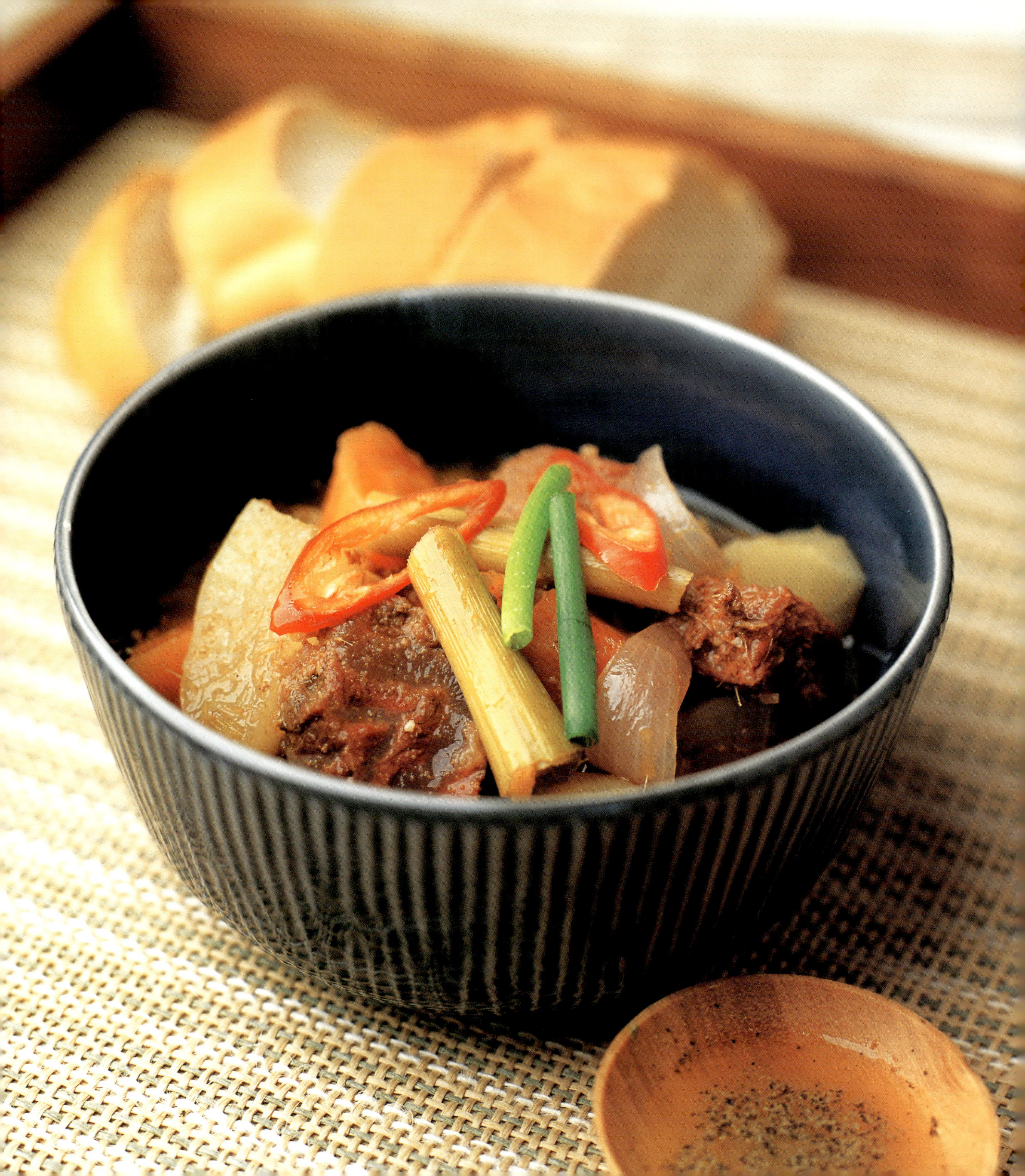

# VIETNAMESE BEEF STEW

Seemingly adapted for the tropics, this wholesome, hearty stew has a refreshingly tangy taste and is not overly rich or heavy.

### Ingredients
| | |
|---|---|
| Beef thigh | 1 kg (2 lb 3 oz), cut into 2-cm (1-inch) cubes or desired bite-sized pieces |
| Cooking oil | 4 Tbsp |
| Sliced shallots | 1 Tbsp |
| Minced garlic | 1 Tbsp |
| Minced lemon grass | 1 Tbsp |
| Lemon grass stalks | 4 |
| Coconut juice | 1 litre (4 cups / 1 3/5 pints) |
| Carrots | 250 g (9 oz), cut into bite-sized pieces |
| White (Chinese) radishes | 250 g (9 oz), cut into bite-sized pieces |
| Onions | 2, peeled and cut into wedges |
| Tomato sauce (ketchup) | 2 Tbsp |
| Chilli sauce | 2 Tbsp |
| Spring onions (scallions) | 5, finely chopped or cut into 5-cm (2-inch) lengths |
| Red chillies | 2, sliced |

### Seasoning
| | |
|---|---|
| Salt | to taste |
| Sugar | to taste |
| Chicken seasoning powder | to taste |

### Marinade (combined)
| | |
|---|---|
| Five-spice powder | 1 tsp |
| Minced garlic | 2 Tbsp |
| Minced shallots | 2 Tbsp |
| Minced lemon grass | 2 Tbsp |
| Pounded ginger | 1 Tbsp |
| Curry powder | 2 Tbsp |
| Chicken seasoning powder | 3 tsp |

## Step-By-Step

A coconut usually contains less than 1 litre (4 cups / 1 3/5 pints) of juice, so pour juice out to measure and derive desired amount.

Pounding peeled ginger slices with a mortar and pestle until fine takes little time and effort.

Adding tomato and chilli sauces to the stew enhances the already rich flavours of the marinade.

### Method
- Marinate beef cubes for 30 minutes.
- Heat oil in a large saucepan. Add shallot slices and minced garlic and lemon grass. Fry until fragrant.
- Add marinated beef and fry until golden brown. Then, add lemon grass stalks and coconut juice. Bring to the boil.
- Discard scum on liquid surface. Cover saucepan and simmer for 45 minutes to 1 hour or until meat is tender.
- Add carrots and radishes and simmer for 10 minutes, then add onion wedges, then tomato and chilli sauces. Return to the boil over high heat. Adjust to taste with seasoning ingredients before removing from heat.
- Garnish with spring onions and chilli slices and serve with dipping sauce (see pg 51).
- Eat dish with sliced French loaf or with flat rice noodles.

## Step-By-Step

The edges of a star fruit are hard and fibrous, so cut off and discard them before slicing into star shapes.

If a greater degree of doneness is preferred at the end of burning, add more alcohol to set alight.

If a star fruit slice is too large, make a couple of slits across the underside so that it will bend with rolling.

# BEEF ON FIRE

A guaranteed spectacle if done at the table, this dish uses gentle cradling heat to cook beef slices to tender perfection.

### Ingredients

| | |
|---|---|
| Beef fillet | 250 g (9 oz), slice thinly and across grain to ensure tenderness |
| Ginger | 50 g (2 oz), peeled and julienned |
| Skinned peanuts (groundnuts) | 50 g (2 oz), roasted and roughly pounded |
| Coriander (cilantro) leaves | 50 g (2 oz) |
| Rice wine | 125 ml (4 fl oz / 1/2 cup), for burning only, at least 40% alcohol (80 proof) |
| Round rice papers | 30 sheets, 15 cm (6 inches) in diameter |
| Chinese lettuce | 1 bunch, leaves separated and washed |
| Pineapple | 1/2, peeled, cored, quartered lengthways and cut into 0.5-cm (1/4-inch) wide slices |
| Sour star fruits | 2, washed, hard edges pared and sliced into star shapes |
| Green bananas (optional) | 2, peeled, sliced into rounds |

### Marinade

| | |
|---|---|
| Lemon grass | 50 g (2 oz), chopped |
| Garlic | 50 g (2 oz), peeled and chopped |
| Five-spice powder | 1/2 tsp |
| Chicken seasoning powder | 1/2 tsp |
| Light soy sauce | 1 tsp |
| Sugar | 1/2 tsp |
| Salt | 1/2 tsp |

### Dipping Sauce (combined)

| | |
|---|---|
| Fish sauce | 1 Tbsp |
| Coconut juice | 2 Tbsp, or boiled water |
| Sugar | 1 tsp |
| Vinegar | 1 Tbsp, or lemon juice |
| Garlic | 1 clove, peeled and minced |
| Red chilli (optional) | 1 or to taste, minced |

### Method

- Prepare marinade. First, fry lemon grass and garlic in a little oil until golden brown. Dish out and combine with remaining marinade ingredients. Marinate beef slices for 30 minutes.
- Put marinated beef in a heatproof (flameproof) or clay bowl. Add ginger, peanuts and coriander on top. Place bowl into a larger heatproof or clay bowl containing the rice wine, then set rice wine alight.
- When fire is extinguished, beef slices should be just cooked. Serve with remaining ingredients and dipping sauce.
- To assemble, place 1 lettuce leaf at the lower end of a rice paper round already smeared with water to soften. Layer on slices of pineapple, star fruit and green banana, if used, and top with beef slices. Fold in left and right sides, then roll up firmly.
- Eat rolls with dipping sauce.

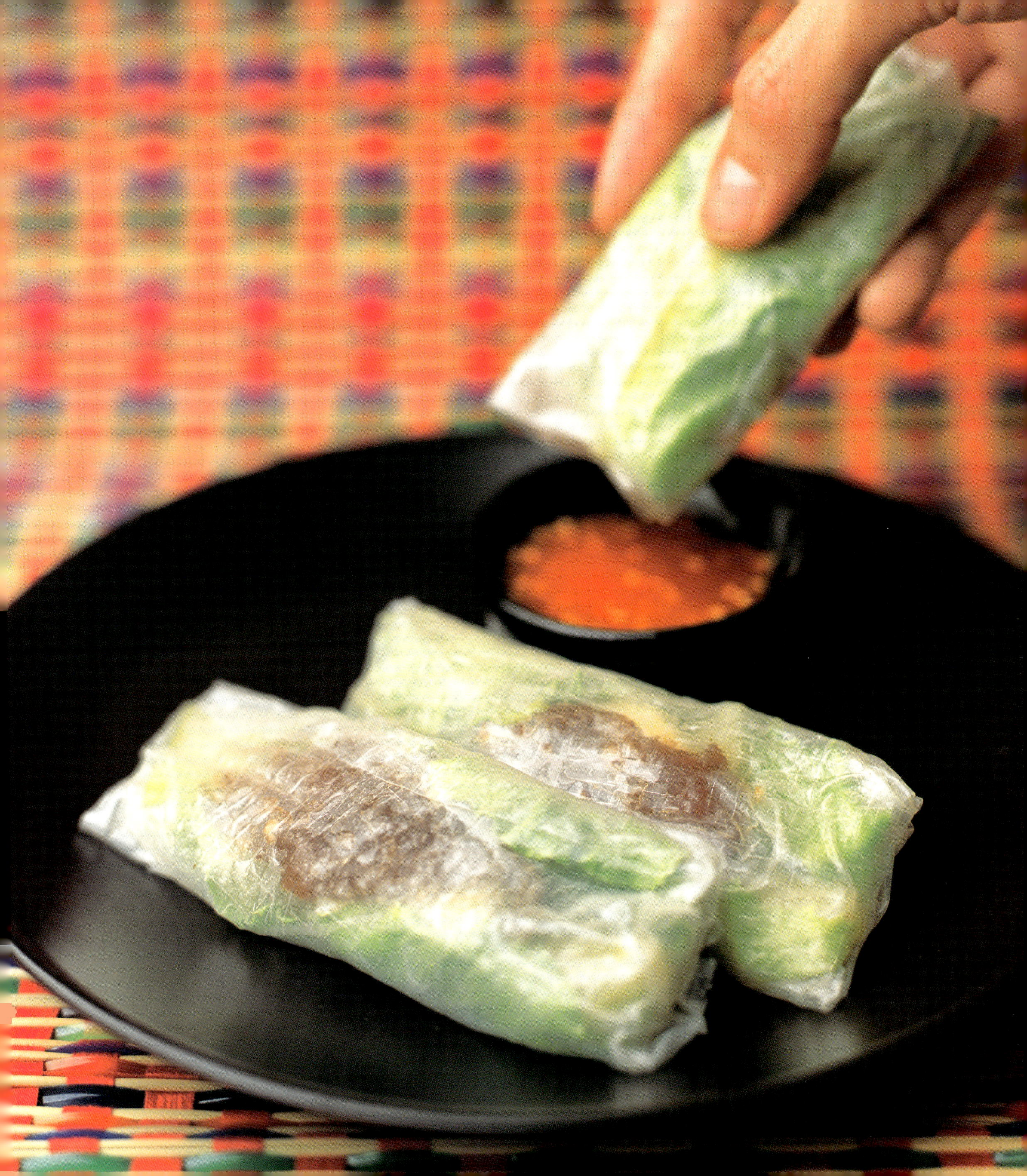

Put all stock ingredients into a pot and bring to the boil, then simmer. The resulting stock should taste sweet and sour.

When arranging beef slices, avoid excessive overlapping so the flavour from the onion slices can infuse.

Stock should be kept simmering hot at the table, either over a small stove or in a fondue pot.

*Step-By-Step*

# BEEF COOKED IN VINEGAR

Slightly different from Beef on Fire, the vinegar stock and the pickled vegetables in this dish provide a more tangy and appetising taste.

### Ingredients

| | |
|---|---|
| Beef fillet | 1 kg (2 lb 3 oz), sliced thinly and across grain to ensure tenderness |
| Onion | 1, peeled and thinly sliced |
| Round rice papers | 30 sheets, 15 cm (6 inches) in diameter |
| Chinese lettuce | 1 bunch, leaves separated, washed and drained |
| Cucumber | 1, washed, peeled, cored and sliced into 5-cm (2-inch) lengths |
| Pickled vegetables | 1 jar, about 200 g (7 oz), consisting of cabbage, carrots and white radishes |
| Sour star fruits | 2, washed, edges trimmed and sliced into star shapes |
| Green bananas (optional) | 2, peeled, sliced into rounds |
| Fresh rice vermicelli | 500 g (1 lb 1½ oz), replaceable with Indian string hoppers (*putu mayam*) or thick round rice (*laksa*) noodles |

### Marinade (combined)

| | |
|---|---|
| Lemon grass | 3 tsp, finely chopped |
| Ground white pepper | 2 tsp |
| Sugar | 1 tsp |
| Chicken seasoning powder | 2 tsp |
| Garlic juice | 2 tsp, extracted by pounding and squeezing garlic cloves |

### Stock (combined)

| | |
|---|---|
| Vinegar | 125 ml (4 fl oz / ½ cup) |
| Coconut juice | 125 ml (4 fl oz / ½ cup) |
| Minced garlic | 1 tsp |
| Ground white pepper | 1 tsp |
| Salt | 1 tsp |
| Sugar | 2 tsp |
| Chicken seasoning powder | 1 tsp |

### Method

- Marinate beef for 30 minutes to 1 hour.
- Meanwhile, prepare stock. Bring combined stock ingredients to the boil, then reduce heat for sustained simmering.
- Arrange beef slices flat on a serving plate or platter. Distribute onion slices on top.
- Serve beef slices with complementary ingredients, dipping sauce and hot stock.
- To assemble, first take some beef slices and dip into hot stock to cook, then drain and set aside. Place 1 lettuce leaf at the lower end of a rice paper round already smeared with water to soften. Layer on cucumber, pickled vegetables, star fruit and green banana, if used. Top with some rice vermicelli and cooked beef, then fold in left and right sides and roll up firmly.
- Eat with rolls and dipping sauce (see pg 70).

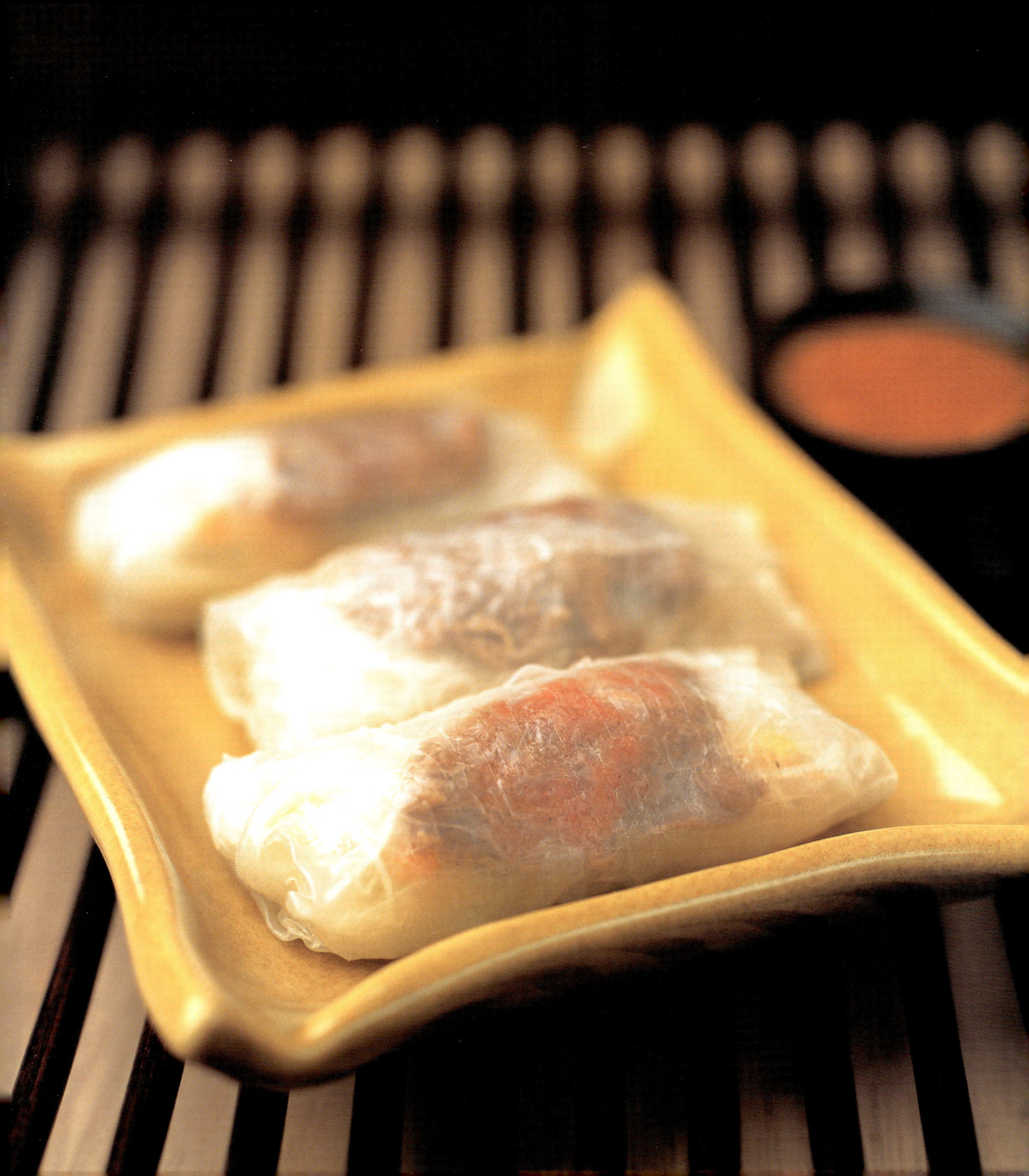

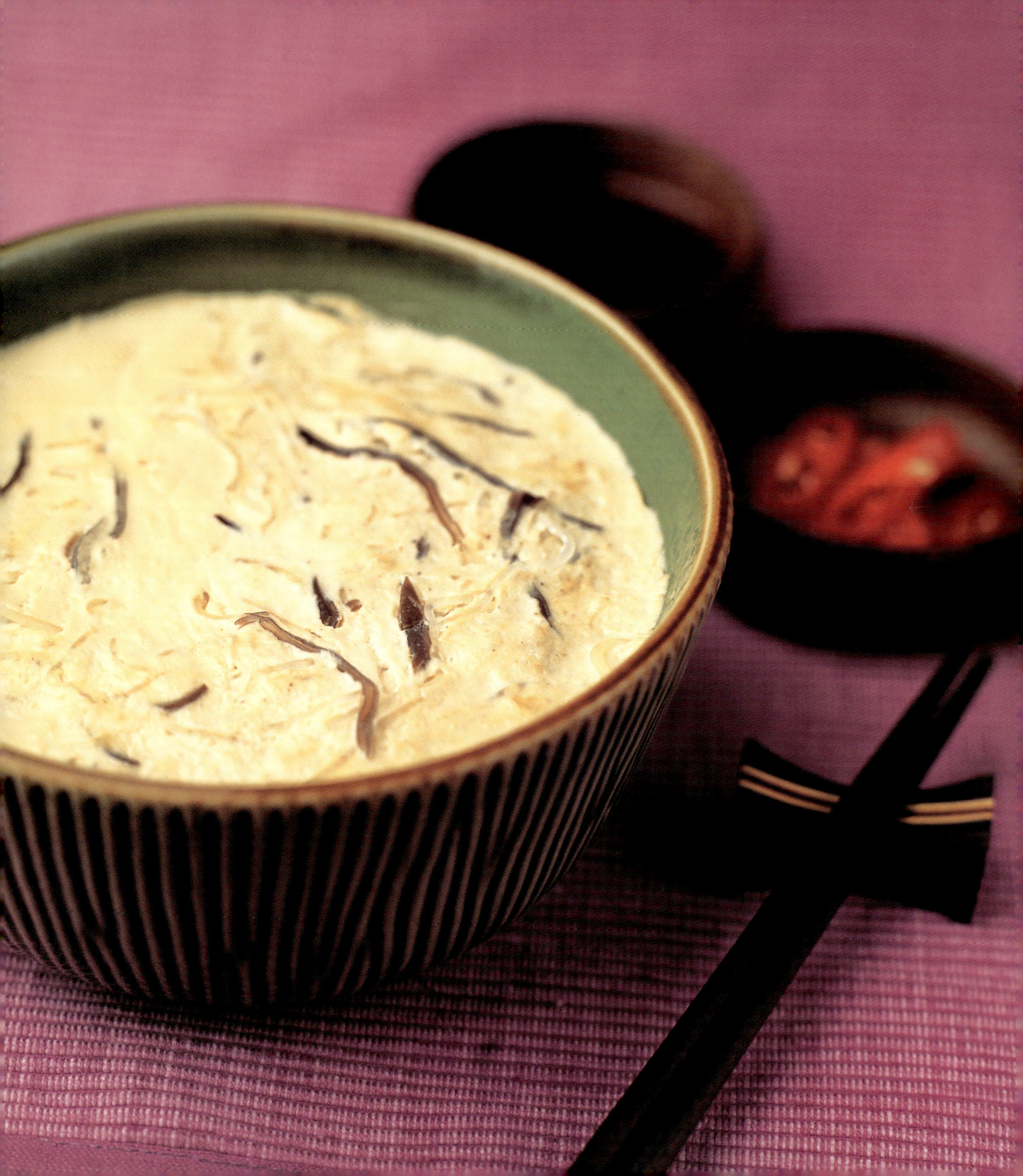

# STEAMED MINCED PORK WITH DUCK EGGS

A dish with Chinese roots, the Vietnamese version differs in using duck eggs, as well as transparent vermicelli and black fungus for crunch.

### Ingredients
| | |
|---|---|
| Cooking oil | 1 tsp |
| Garlic | 1 clove, peeled and minced |
| Minced lean pork | 300 g (10½ oz) |
| Transparent (glass) vermicelli | 5 g (⅙ oz), soaked in water for 10 minutes then drained and cut into 1-cm (½-inch) pieces |
| Dried black (wood ear) fungus | 3, soaked to soften and hard stems discarded |
| Duck eggs | 3, lightly beaten |
| Light soy sauce | 2 Tbsp |
| Red chilli slices | 2 Tbsp |

### Seasoning
| | |
|---|---|
| Ground black pepper | 1 tsp |
| Sugar | 1 tsp |
| Salt | ½ tsp |
| Cooking oil | 1 tsp |

### Step-By-Step

Soak transparent vermicelli in plenty of water to reconstitute and drain before use.

Lightly beat the duck eggs to mix the yolks and whites.

When all the ingredients are well mixed, steam over rapidly boiling water for about 30 minutes.

### Method

- Heat oil in a saucepan. Fry chopped garlic until golden brown. Dish out and set aside.
- Combine minced pork, vermicelli, black fungus, eggs and fried garlic in a heatproof (flameproof) bowl. Mix well.
- Add seasoning ingredients to meat mixture. Mix well again.
- Steam bowl for 30 minutes.
- Serve dish with soy sauce in a small saucer and chilli slices in another.

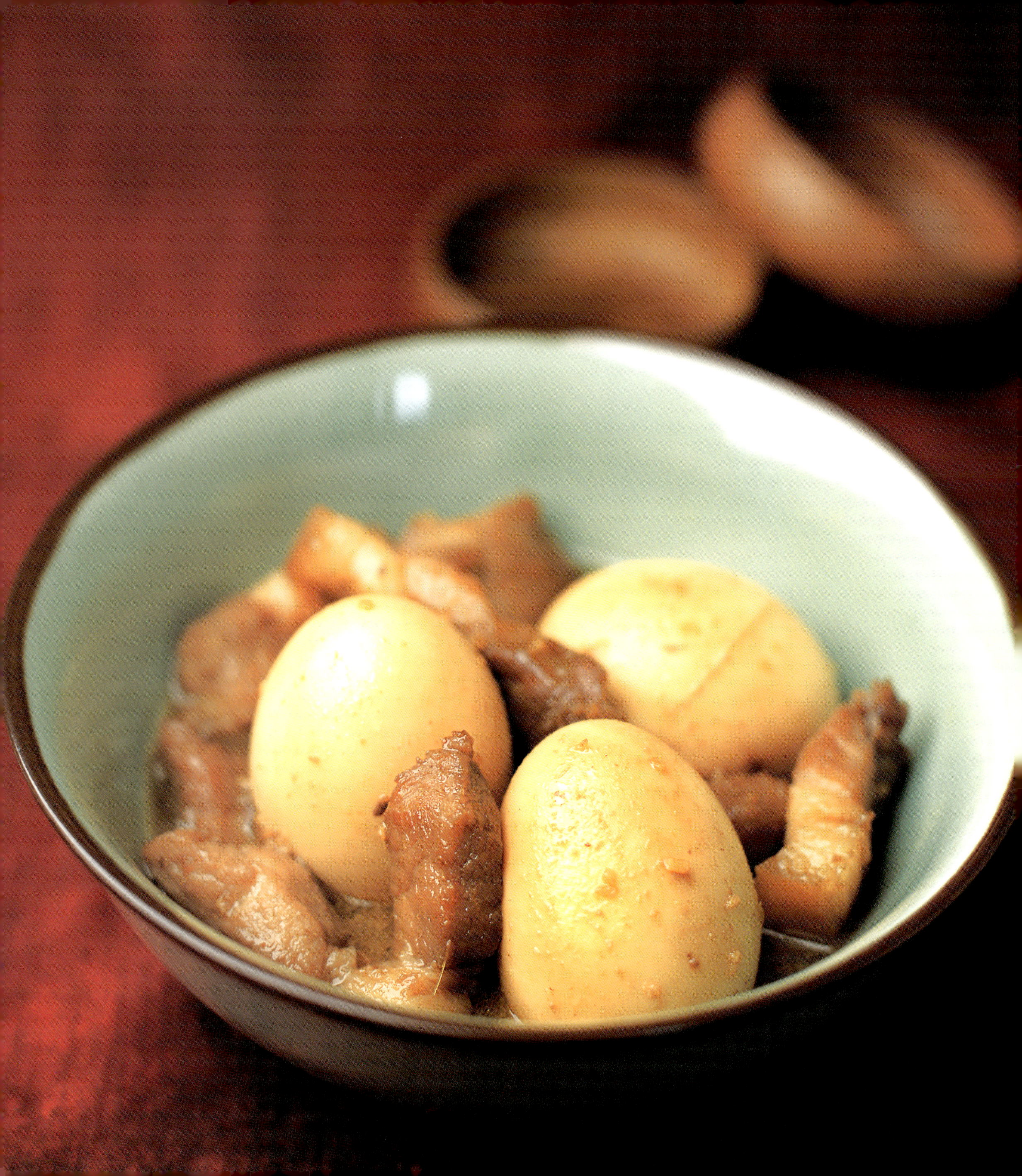

# PORK STEWED IN COCONUT JUICE

Aside from tender and smooth pork pieces, the hard-boiled eggs, in having absorbed the flavours of the gravy, also make tasty nourishment.

### Ingredients

| | |
|---|---|
| Pork thigh | 1 kg (2 lb 3 oz), with some skin and fat intact |
| Eggs | 3–4 |
| Coconut juice | 1 litre (4 cups / 1 3/5 pints) |

### Marinade (combined)

| | |
|---|---|
| Fish sauce | 125 ml (4 fl oz / 1/2 cup) |
| Salt (optional) | 1/2 Tbsp |
| Brown sugar | 4 tsp |
| Minced garlic | 2 tsp |

## Step-By-Step

Cut pork into chunks or desired stewing size. If too thin, pork pieces will fall apart with cooking.

To make hard-boiled eggs, put them into a pot of cold water and bring to the boil. Then, simmer for 7–8 minutes.

To ensure a rich flavour, pork and marinade must be cooked until almost dried up before coconut juice is added.

### Method

- Wash and cut pork into bite-sized pieces, then marinate them for 1 hour.
- Meanwhile, prepare hard-boiled eggs. When eggs are cooked, transfer them to a bowl of room-temperature water to cool, then shell them.
- Cook pork and marinade in a pot until liquid is almost dried up. Stir occasionally.
- Pour in coconut juice and add eggs. Return to the boil, all the while discarding scum from liquid surface to keep gravy clear. When liquid reaches the boil, reduce heat and simmer until pork is lightly golden.
- When done, pork should be tender but not too soft; fat and skin would have separated a little from meat.

Cut off the legs of each frog at the joints, as one would chicken thighs and wings.

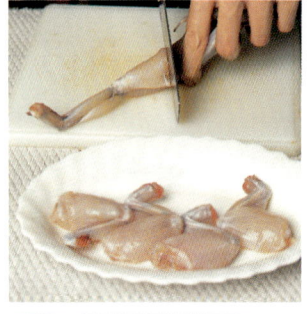

Combine marinade ingredients in a bowl and mix well before adding to meat for more even flavouring.

Add remaining coconut milk only when frog pieces are cooked through. Excessive boiling of coconut milk draws out oil.

*Step-By-Step*

# STIR-FRIED FROG IN COCONUT MILK

This dish smells and looks like a mild curry, but the use of frog meat is what distinguishes it from curries of other cuisines.

### Ingredients

| | |
|---|---|
| Frogs | 1 kg (2 lb 3 oz), washed, skinned and with legs separated from bodies |
| Cooking oil | 1–2 Tbsp |
| Minced garlic | 1 tsp |
| Preserved soy bean paste | 2 tsp |
| Coconut milk | 500 ml (16 fl oz / 2 cups) |
| Water | 500 ml (16 fl oz / 2 cups) |
| Skinned peanuts (groundnuts) | 50 g (2 oz), roasted and roughly pounded |
| Coriander (cilantro) leaves for garnishing | |
| Fish sauce | 2 Tbsp |
| Red chilli slices | 2 Tbsp |

### Seasoning

| | |
|---|---|
| Salt | to taste |
| Ground black pepper | to taste |
| Chicken seasoning powder | to taste |

### Marinade (combined)

| | |
|---|---|
| Minced lemon grass | 4 tsp |
| Curry powder | 2 tsp |
| Five-spice powder | 1 tsp |
| Sesame seed oil | 1 tsp |
| Ground black pepper | 1 tsp |
| Salt | 2 tsp |
| Sugar | 1 tsp |
| Chicken seasoning powder | 1 tsp |

### Method

- Marinate frog pieces for 30 minutes.
- Heat oil in a cooking pan or wok. Add garlic and fry until golden brown. Add frog pieces and stir quickly.
- Add preserved soy bean paste, 125 ml (4 fl oz / 1/2 cup) coconut milk and water. Cover pan to cook frog pieces. When cooked through, add remaining coconut milk and bring to the boil. Adjust to taste with seasoning ingredients before removing from heat.
- To serve, dish out and garnish with peanuts and coriander. Serve with fish sauce in 1 small saucer and sliced chillies in another.

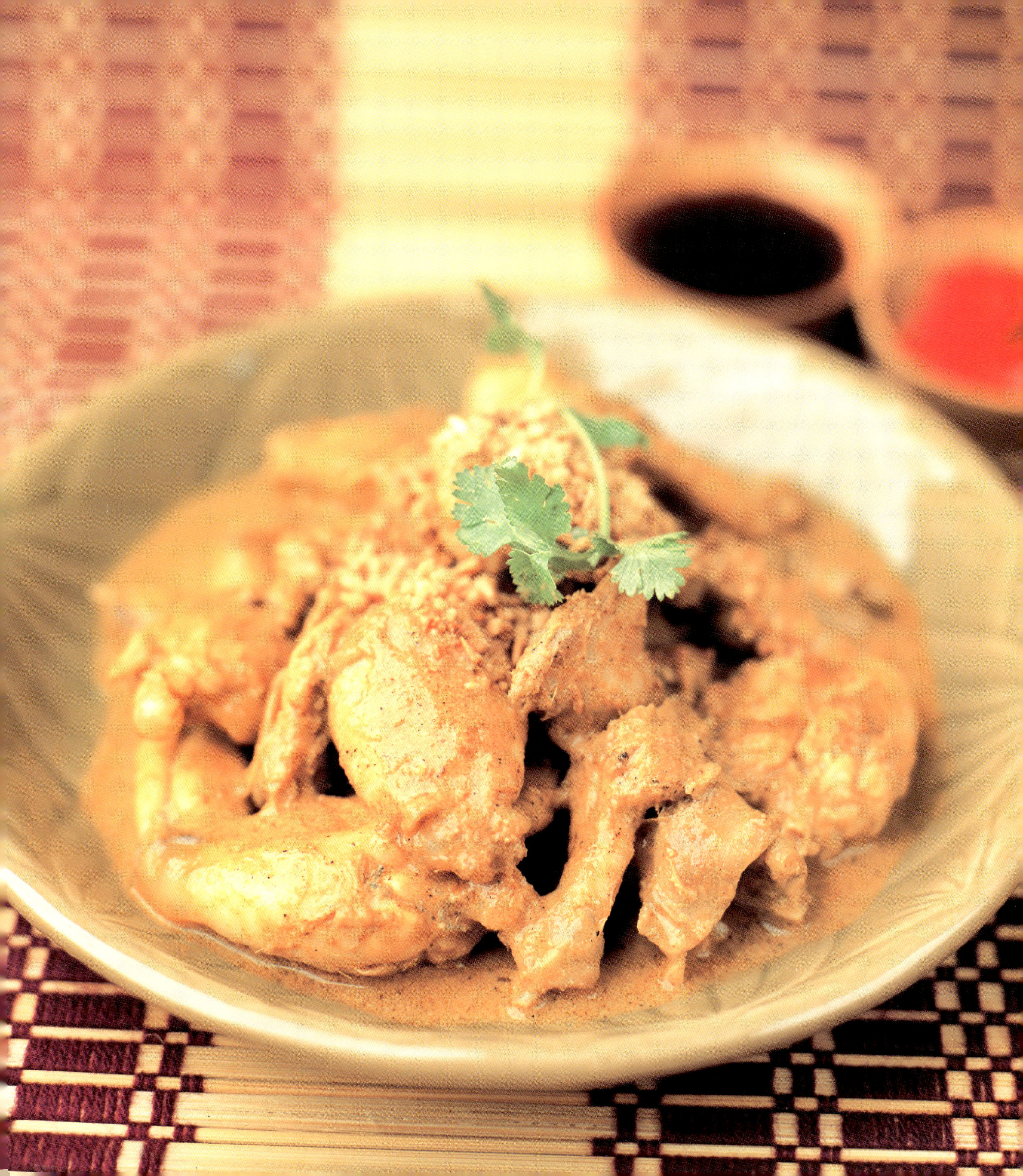

Traditional Chicken Noodle Soup

Beef Noodles

Duck Noodle Soup

Crabmeat Noodle Soup

Duck Cooked in Fermented Bean Curd

Saigon Fish Congee

Quang Noodles

Eel Noodles

RICE & NOODLES

Of stock ingredients, put ginger, shallots, cinnamon and star anise into a small cloth bag and tie it up.

To cool down chicken skin, one could lower the bird into a basin of water or position it under a running tap.

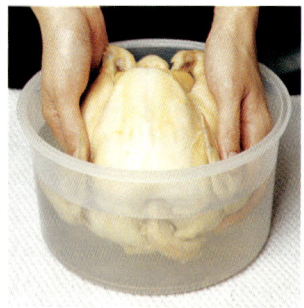

Put rice noodles and bean sprouts into a wire strainer, then lower into boiling water to blanch.

*Step-By-Step*

# TRADITIONAL CHICKEN NOODLE SOUP

Served with rice noodles, this chicken soup is old-fashioned wholesome and comforting.

### Ingredients

| | |
|---|---|
| Stock* | 1 recipe (see pg 83) |
| Chicken | 1, whole, about 1.5 kg (3 lb 4½ oz) |
| Sesame seed oil | as required |
| Thin flat rice noodles | 2 kg (4 lb 6 oz) |
| Bean sprouts | 200 g (7 oz), tailed if preferred |
| Chopped spring onions (scallions) | 50 g (2 oz) |
| Onions | 2, peeled and thinly sliced |
| Preserved soy bean paste | 5 g (⅙ oz) |
| Chilli sauce | 5 g (⅙ oz) |
| Limes | 4, quartered and cored |

### Seasoning

| | |
|---|---|
| Salt | ¼ tsp |
| Ground white pepper | ¼ tsp |
| Chicken seasoning powder | ¼ tsp |

### Method

- Prepare stock. When ready, lower in chicken and leave to boil over medium heat for about 30 minutes.
- Drain cooked chicken from stock, then lower it into a basin of water for 1 minute to cool down skin.
- Smear sesame seed oil onto cooled chicken skin, then chop oiled chicken into bite-sized pieces and set aside.
- Strain stock and discard solid ingredients. Return liquid to the boil, then add seasoning ingredients. Leave soup to simmer.
- Put desired amounts of noodles and bean sprouts into a wire mesh strainer. Blanch in boiling hot water, drain and transfer to individual serving bowls.
- Add desired amounts of cooked chicken pieces, chopped spring onions and onion slices on top of noodles in each bowl, then ladle boiling soup over.
- Serve noodles with small saucers of preserved soy bean paste, chilli sauce, and lime quarters.

**\*Stock**

| | |
|---|---|
| Ginger | 50 g (2 oz), roasted until golden brown, peeled and slightly crushed |
| Shallots | 100 g (3 1/2 oz), roasted until golden brown and peeled |
| Cinnamon sticks | 10 g (1/3 oz) |
| Star anise | 5 |
| Chicken bones | 500 g (1 lb 1 1/2 oz), washed in salted water and drained well before use |
| Chicken fat | 100 g (3 1/2 oz) |
| White (Chinese) radishes | 2, about 200 g (7 oz) each, peeled and roughly cut |
| Water | 5 litres (20 cups / 8 pints) |

**Method**
- Put ginger, shallots, cinnamon and star anise into a small cloth bag and tie it up.
- In a large pot, bring cloth bag, chicken bones and fat, radishes and water to the boil, then simmer over low heat for 1 hour 30 minutes. Regularly remove scum from surface to keep stock clear.

### *Stock

| | |
|---|---|
| Onion | 1, large, roasted until golden (slightly burnt), peeled and lightly pounded |
| Ginger | 5-cm (2-inch) knob, roasted until golden (slightly burnt), peeled and lightly pounded |
| Cinnamon sticks | 2 |
| Star anise | 3 |
| Beef bones | 1 kg (2 lb 3 oz), washed, boiled in water, strained and liquid discarded, or beef stock granules if beef bones are unavailable |
| Water | 5 litres (20 cups / 8 pints) |

### Method
- Of stock ingredients, put roasted onion and ginger, cinnamon and star anise into a small cloth bag and tie it up.
- In a large pot, combine cloth bag, beef bones and water. Bring to the boil, then simmer over low heat for 2 hours 15 minutes. Regularly remove scum from liquid surface to keep stock clear.

# BEEF NOODLES

This is a classic Vietnamese meal of beef slices and rice noodles bathed in a clear soup that belies its rich flavour.

### Ingredients
| | |
|---|---|
| Stock* | 1 recipe (see pg 84) |
| Beef thigh | 400 g (14 oz), with some ligaments, washed and dried |
| Beef fillet | 400 g (14 oz), washed and thinly sliced across grain |
| Thin flat rice noodles | 2 kg (4 lb 6 oz) |
| Bean sprouts | 200 g (7 oz), washed and drained well |
| Spring onions (scallions) | 2–3 stalks, finely chopped |
| Onion | 1, large, peeled and thinly sliced |
| Preserved soy bean paste | 5 g (1/6 oz) |
| Chilli sauce | 5 g (1/6 oz) |
| Limes | 4, quartered and cored |

### Seasoning
| | |
|---|---|
| Salt | 1/4 tsp |
| Ground white pepper | 1/4 tsp |
| Chicken seasoning powder | 1/4 tsp |

**Step-By-Step**

Simmer stock ingredients — cloth bag of spices, beef bones and water — for approximately 2 hours.

On top of blanched noodles and bean sprouts, arrange desired number of raw and cooked beef slices.

When satisfied with all the topping ingredients, ladle boiling hot soup over.

### Method
- Prepare stock. When ready, add in beef thigh and simmer for 45 minutes or until ligaments soften. Then, drain beef thigh and thinly slice when cooled.
- Strain stock and discard solid ingredients. Return liquid to the boil, then add seasoning ingredients. Leave soup to simmer.
- Put desired amounts of noodles and bean sprouts into a wire mesh strainer and blanch in boiling water to heat up ingredients, then transfer to individual serving bowls.
- On top of noodles in each bowl, arrange raw beef fillet slices and cooked beef thigh slices, as well as add on chopped spring onions and onion slices. Ladle boiling soup over and raw beef will cook in the meantime.
- Serve noodles with small saucers of preserved soy bean paste, chilli sauce and lime quarters.

**Dipping Sauce**

| | |
|---|---|
| Finely chopped ginger | 1 Tbsp |
| Finely chopped garlic | 2 tsp |
| Finely chopped chilli | 1 tsp |
| Sugar | 2 Tbsp |
| Lime juice | 1 Tbsp |
| Fish sauce | 1 Tbsp |
| Warm water | 125 ml (4 fl oz / 1/2 cup) |

**Method**

- To make dipping sauce, pound chopped garlic and ginger together, then transfer to a bowl. Add all remaining ingredients and mix well. Sauce should taste sweet, sour and salty.

# DUCK NOODLE SOUP

A hearty meal of bamboo shoot slices and duck pieces dusted with shallot slices and peanuts in a soupy bed of noodles.

### Ingredients

| | |
|---|---|
| Duck | 1, about 2 kg (4 lb 6 oz), washed, neck and feet discarded and halved lengthways |
| Lime juice | 1 Tbsp |
| Minced ginger | 1 Tbsp |
| Minced garlic | 1 Tbsp |
| Chicken seasoning powder | 3 tsp or more to taste |
| Chicken stock | 2 litres (8 cups / 3$\frac{1}{5}$ pints) |
| Dried or canned bamboo shoots | 300 g (10$\frac{1}{2}$ oz), soaked in water overnight and drained before use if dried and sliced if fresh |
| Salt | to taste |
| Shallots | 100 g (3$\frac{1}{2}$ oz), peeled, sliced and crisp-fried |
| Skinned peanuts (groundnuts) | 100 g (3$\frac{1}{2}$ oz), coarsely ground |
| Fresh rice vermicelli | 2 kg (4 lb 6 oz), or 500 g (1 lb 1$\frac{1}{2}$ oz) dried rice vermicelli soaked in water to soften and drained |
| Bean sprouts | 300 g (10$\frac{1}{2}$ oz) |
| Spring onions (scallions) | 100 g (3$\frac{1}{2}$ oz), chopped |
| Polygonum (*laksa*) leaves | 50 g (2 oz), washed, stems discarded and leaves coarsely chopped |

## Step-By-Step

If preferred, pinch off heads and tails of bean sprouts to improve presentation.

To make chicken stock, boil 1 kg (2 lb 3 oz) of bones in 3 litres (12 cups / 4$\frac{4}{5}$ pints) of water for 30 minutes. Regularly remove scum.

As tastes and appetites vary from person to person, adjust noodle, meat and topping amounts to suit diner's preferences.

### Method

- Rub duck with combined lime juice and ginger combined to remove any unpleasant smell. Then, wash duck, drain and season with garlic and seasoning powder.
- Bring stock to the boil, then lower in duck. Leave to cook for 15–20 minutes, then drain and set aside.
- Add bamboo shoot slices to stock and return to the boil. Adjust to taste with seasoning powder and salt if desired. Leave to simmer.
- Chop cooked duck into bite-sized pieces and arrange on a plate. Sprinkle on some fried shallot slices and ground peanuts.
- Blanch noodles and bean sprouts, then transfer to individual serving bowls. Add some duck pieces, fried shallot slices, chopped spring onions and polygonum leaves on top. Ladle boiling soup over.
- Serve noodles with dipping sauce (see pg 86).

# CRABMEAT NOODLE SOUP

The sweetness of crabmeat is given centre stage in this noodle dish supported by straw mushrooms and a thickened pork stock.

### Ingredients

| | |
|---|---|
| Stock* | 1 recipe (see pg 89) |
| Cooking oil | 1 Tbsp |
| Chopped garlic | 2 Tbsp |
| Crabmeat | 300 g (10 1/2 oz) |
| Salt | 1/2 tsp |
| Ground white pepper | 1/2 tsp |
| Fresh or canned straw mushrooms | 200 g (7 oz), each halved or sliced into thirds lengthways |
| Thick round rice (*laksa*) noodles | 1.5 kg (3 lb 4 1/2 oz) |
| Shallots | 30 g (1 oz), peeled, sliced and crisp-fried |
| Spring onions (scallions) | 50 g (2 oz), chopped |
| Fish sauce | 2 Tbsp |
| Sliced chillies | 2 Tbsp |
| Limes | 3, quartered and cores discarded |

### Seasoning

| | |
|---|---|
| Chicken seasoning powder | 1/2 tsp |
| Ground black pepper | 1/2 tsp |
| Salt | 1/2 tsp |

**Step-By-Step**

While stock is boiling, prepare crispy fried shallot slices in the meantime.

When adding green bean flour to clear stock, stir it in bit by bit to avoid clumps.

Fresh straw mushrooms cook easily, while canned ones are already edible, so be careful not to overcook.

### Method

- Prepare stock.
- Heat oil in a wok or skillet (frying pan). Add 1 Tbsp garlic and stir-fry until fragrant. Add crabmeat and sauté for a few minutes. Season crabmeat with salt and pepper. Dish out crabmeat to a plate.
- Add remaining garlic to wok. When fragrant, sauté mushrooms for a few minutes, then dish out.
- Put desired amounts of noodles into individual serving bowls and add some crabmeat and straw mushrooms on top. Ladle boiling soup over, then sprinkle on crispy fried shallots and chopped spring onions.
- Serve hot with some fish sauce, chilli slices and lime quarters in separate saucers.

**Stock*

| | |
|---|---|
| Pork bones | 1 kg (2 lb 3 oz), washed |
| White (Chinese) radish | 1, peeled and cut into bite-sized pieces |
| Water | 3 litres (12 cups / 4⅘ pints) |
| Green (mung) bean flour | 1 Tbsp |

**Method**
- Boil pork bones and radish in water for 1 hour. Regularly remove scum from liquid surface to get a clear stock.
- When ready, strain stock and discard bones and radish. Add green bean flour to thicken liquid, then add seasoning ingredients.
- Sustain liquid at the boil.

Peel yam with a sharp cleaver. Yams tend to have hard skins.

To save some time, prepare dipping sauce while waiting for yam pieces to cook and soften.

When ready to serve, transfer soup to a steamboat (*right*) or an electric hot pot to sustain at the boil at the table.

*Step-By-Step*

# DUCK COOKED IN FERMENTED BEAN CURD

Duck, red fermented bean curd and coconut milk come together to spike the tongue with a series of forward flavours.

### Ingredients

| | |
|---|---|
| Duck | 1, whole, 1.5–2 kg (3 lb 4½ oz–4 lb 6 oz) |
| Rice wine | 2 Tbsp |
| Ginger | 1 large knob, about 50 g (2 oz), peeled and pounded until fine |
| Coconut milk | about 400 ml (12½ fl oz) |
| Water | 500 ml (16 fl oz / 2 cups) |
| Yam (taro) | 500 g (1 lb 1½ oz), peeled and cut to bite-sized pieces |
| Salt | 1 pinch or to taste |
| Chicken seasoning powder | ½ tsp or to taste |
| Steamed rice | 1 kg (2 lb 3 oz), or fresh rice vermicelli |
| Water convolvulus | 500 g (1 lb 1½ oz), leaves separated and stems cut into 4-cm (2-inch) lengths |

### *Marinade (combined)*

| | |
|---|---|
| Ground black pepper | ½ tsp |
| Salt | 1 tsp |
| Oyster sauce | 1 tsp |
| Red fermented bean curd | 50 g (2 oz) |
| Sugar | 1 Tbsp |
| Chopped garlic | 1 Tbsp, fried until golden brown |

### *Dipping Sauce*

| | |
|---|---|
| Red fermented bean curd | 50 g (2 oz) |
| Sugar | 3 tsp |
| Coarsely chopped garlic | 1 Tbsp, fried until golden brown |

### Method

- Rub duck all over with rice wine and ginger combined. Set aside for 15 minutes, then rinse and drain. Chop duck into bite-sized pieces and marinate them for 15 minutes.
- Bring coconut milk and water to boil. Add duck pieces and cook over low heat for 15 minutes. Then, add yam and simmer until soft.
- Meanwhile, prepare dipping sauce. Blend red fermented bean curd and sugar together until well combined. Then, stir in fried chopped garlic. Set aside.
- Adjust soup to taste with salt and seasoning powder. Sustain soup at a slow boil.
- To serve, spoon steamed rice into individual serving bowls. Blanch some greens in hot soup to add on top. Drain and add some duck and yam pieces, then ladle on soup. Eat with dipping sauce.

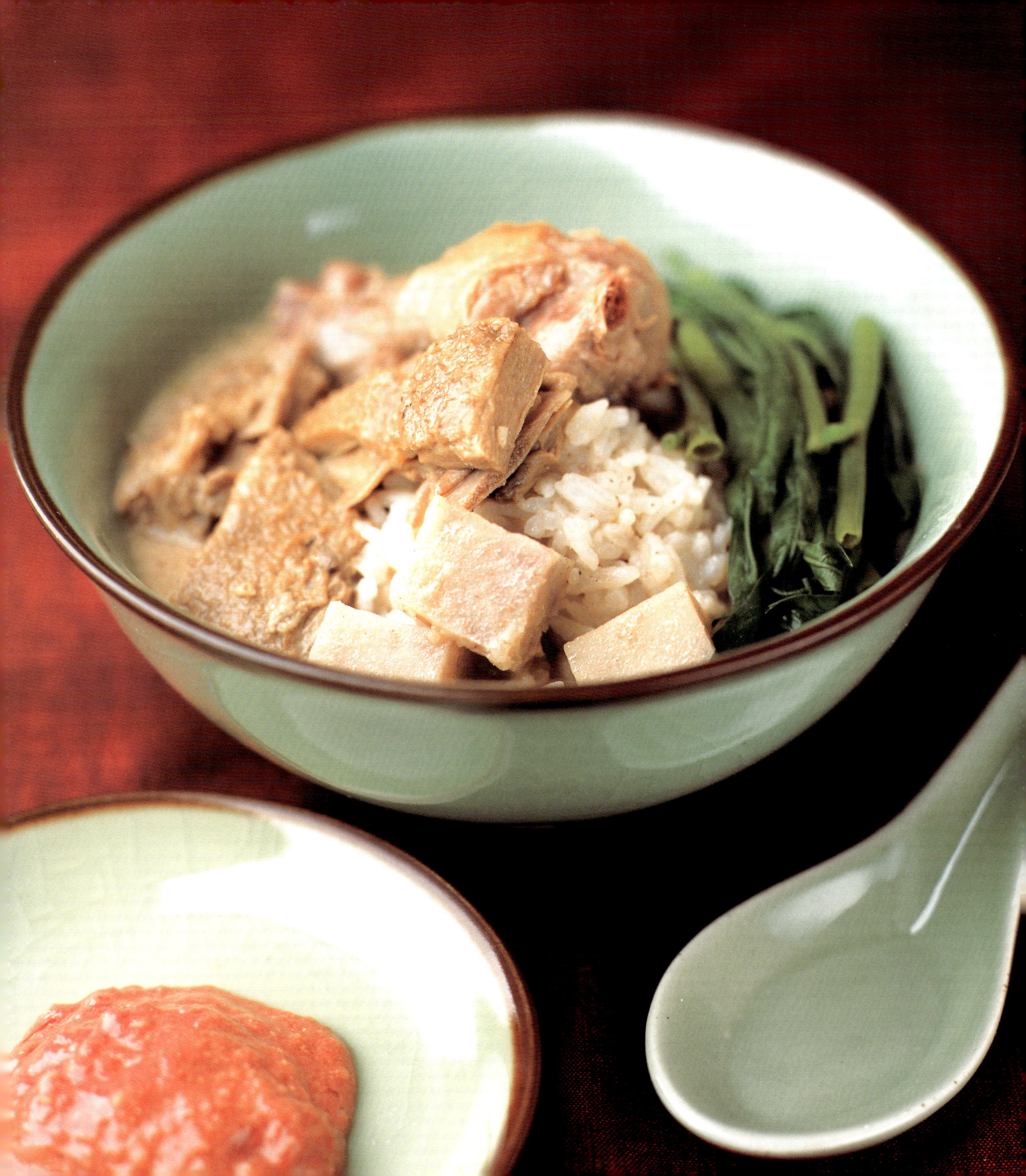

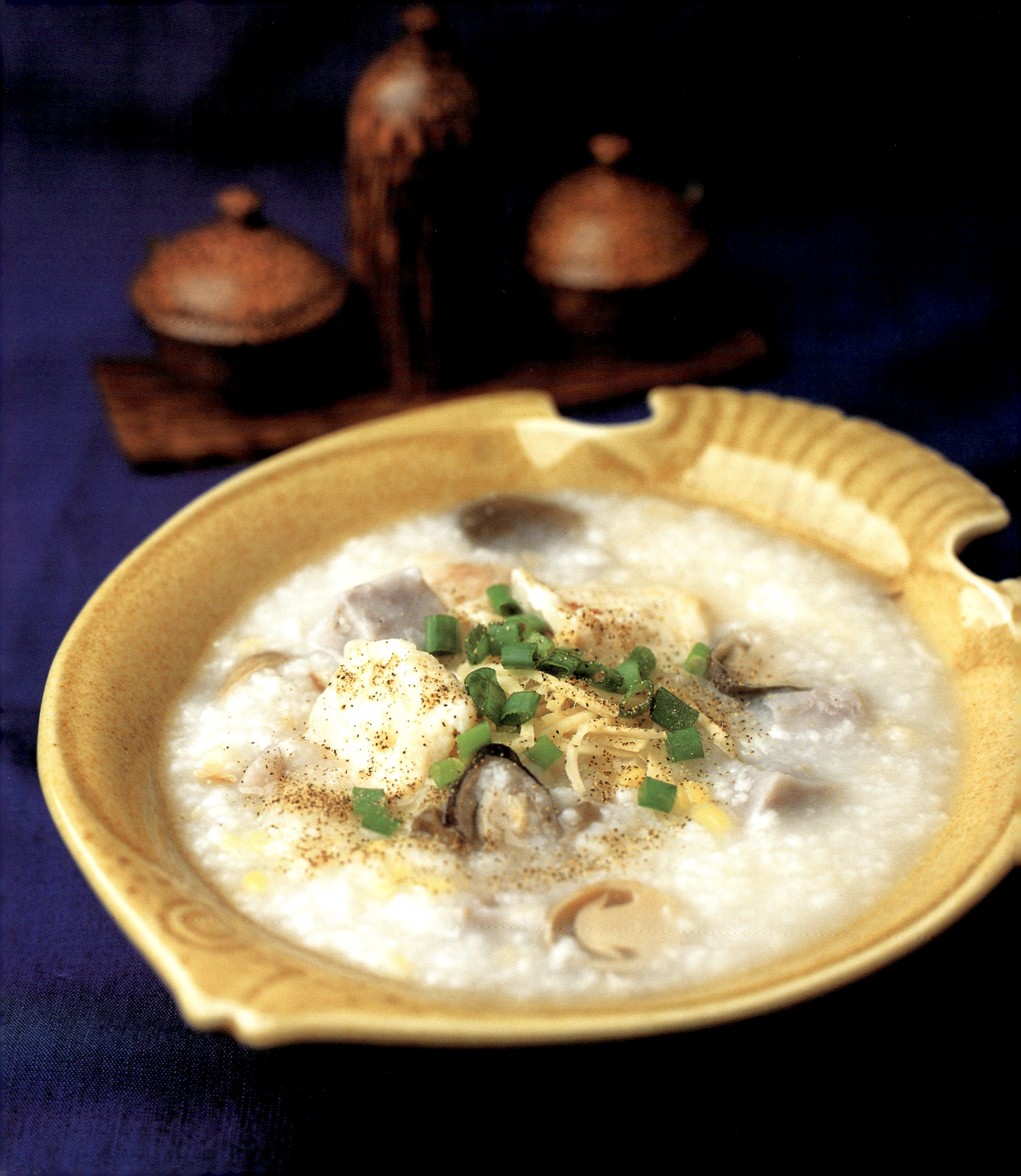

# SAIGON FISH CONGEE

The Vietnamese touch of adding yam cubes and green beans to Chinese fish congee provides for a nutty aroma and more complex texture.

### Ingredients

| | |
|---|---|
| Mud fish, red snapper or sea bass | 1.3 kg (2 lb 13 oz), washed |
| Water | 2.5 litres (10 cups / 4 pints) |
| Fragrant rice | 1 cup, washed and lightly roasted |
| Green (mung) beans | 150 g (5½ oz), soaked in water for 1 hour or until softened and skins discarded |
| Yam (taro) | 300 g (10½ oz), washed, peeled and cut into large cubes |
| Straw mushrooms | 200 g (7 oz) |
| Bean sprouts | 200 g (7 oz), washed and drained well |
| Chopped spring onions (scallions) | 3 Tbsp |
| Ginger | 2-cm (1-inch) knob, peeled and shredded |
| Ground black pepper | ½ tsp |

### Seasoning

| | |
|---|---|
| Crisp-fried shallots | 4 tsp |
| Sesame seed oil | 2 tsp |
| Salt | 2 tsp |
| Chicken seasoning powder | 3 tsp |

## Step-By-Step

With soaking, green beans tend to separate from their skins, which will rise to the top. Remove the rest by rubbing off.

When cutting skinless fish fillets, be sure to slice relatively thickly. Thin slices will disintegrate without skins to hold them together.

Do not blanch or parboil bean sprouts. The hot porridge that blankets them will cook them by the time they reach the table.

### Method

- Skin, bone and fillet fish. Reserve skin and bones for stock. Slice fillets.
- Put fish slices in a bowl. Add seasoning ingredients, mix and set aside for 15 minutes.
- In a pot, combine fish skin and bones and water. Bring to the boil, then lower heat and simmer for 30 minutes.
- Strain stock and discard solid ingredients. Add rice to stock and cook for 1 hour until rice softens.
- Add green beans and yam. Simmer for 15 minutes. Then, add fish slices and mushrooms. Simmer for 5 minutes more or until the fish is cooked through.
- Put some bean sprouts into individual serving bowls. Ladle hot porridge over.
- Top with desired amounts of chopped spring onions, shredded ginger and ground black pepper before serving.

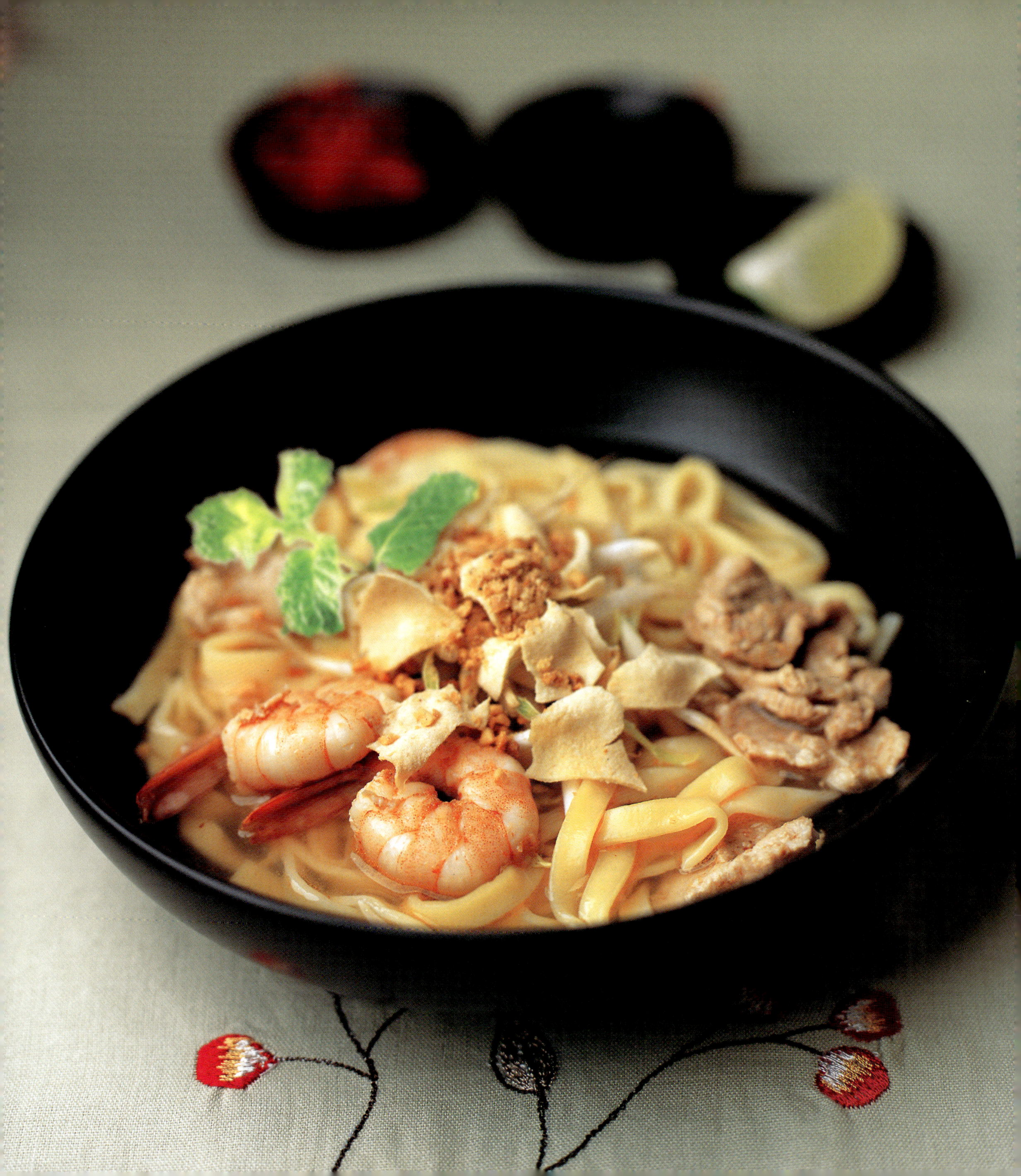

# QUANG NOODLES

A satisfying meal of spicy pork slices and juicy prawns resting on a bed of yellow noodles and dusted with crushed crackers and peanuts.

### Ingredients

| | |
|---|---|
| Prawns (shrimps) | 500 g (1 lb 1½ oz), washed, peeled but with tails intact and deveined |
| Chilli powder | 1 tsp |
| Salt | ½ tsp + 1 pinch |
| Spring onions (scallions) | 50 g (2 oz), chopped |
| Cooking oil | 100 ml (3½ fl oz) |
| Minced garlic | 1 tsp |
| Minced onion | 1 tsp |
| Pork thigh | 300 g (10½ oz), thinly sliced |
| Pork stock | from boiling 1 kg (2 lb 3 oz) pork bones in 2 litres (8 cups / 3⅕ pints) water for 1–2 hours |
| Fish sauce | ½ tsp + 2 Tbsp |
| Chicken seasoning powder | ½ tsp |
| Fresh flat yellow noodles | 500 g (1 lb 1½ oz) |
| Bean sprouts | 100 g (3½ oz) |
| Mint leaves | 50 g (2 oz) |
| Roasted sesame cracker | 1, 30 x 30 cm (12 x 12 inches), coarsely crushed |
| Skinned peanuts (groundnuts) | 100 g (3½ oz), roasted and coarsely ground |
| Red chillies | 2, sliced |
| Limes | 3, quartered and cored |

**Step-By-Step**

Devein peeled prawns (see pg 60), then pinch off sharp tips at the centre of tails to avoid poking diners. The larger the prawn the greater the necessity.

If sesame crackers are unavailable, coarsely crush a few papadums to substitute.

It is important to stir-fry pork slices for 5 minutes before adding prawns. This is because prawns cook more easily than pork.

### Method

- Put prawns into a bowl. Add ½ tsp each of chilli powder and salt and spring onions. Mix well and set aside.
- Heat oil in a pot. Fry garlic and onion until golden over medium heat. Add remaining chilli powder and pork slices. Stir-fry for 5 minutes. Add prawns and stir-fry for 5 minutes more.
- Pour in stock then bring to the boil. Remove scum from liquid surface. Season with 1 pinch salt, ½ tsp fish sauce and seasoning powder.
- Put desired amounts of noodles and bean sprouts into individual serving bowls. Top with desired amount of mint leaves. Ladle boiling soup over, then sprinkle on crushed crackers and ground peanuts.
- Serve hot with 2 Tbsp fish sauce, chilli slices and lime quarters in separate small saucers.

*Stock*

| | |
|---|---|
| Eel bones | as reserved |
| Pork bones | 500 g (1 lb 1½ oz), washed |
| Water | 3 litres (12 cups / 4⅘ pints) |
| Salt | 3 tsp |
| Ground black pepper | 3 tsp |
| Sugar | 2 tsp |
| Chicken seasoning powder | 1 Tbsp |

**Method**
- In a large pot, combine eel and pork bones, as well as water. Bring to the boil, then simmer over low heat for 2 hours.
- Strain stock and discard bones. Season with remaining ingredients. Adjust to taste if necessary. Sustain soup at a slow boil.
- If soup is prepared well in advance, remember to return to the boil before serving.

# EEL NOODLES

A rich tapestry of tastes, colours and textures, this noodle dish takes some preparation but is well worth the effort.

### Ingredients

| | |
|---|---|
| Eel | 1, about 1 kg (2 lb 3 oz), washed |
| Chopped garlic | 1 Tbsp |
| Chopped spring onions (scallions) | 1/2 Tbsp |
| Chopped lemon grass | 2 Tbsp |
| Curry powder | 1/2 tsp |
| Salt | 2 tsp |
| Ground black pepper | 2 tsp |
| Sugar | 3 tsp |
| Chicken seasoning powder | 4 Tbsp |
| Cooking oil | 1 Tbsp |
| Chopped shallots | 1/2 Tbsp |
| Lean pork | 150 g (5 1/3 oz), minced |
| Fermented prawn (shrimp) paste (optional) | 100 g (3 1/2 oz) |
| Bean sprouts | 200 g (7 oz), washed and drained |
| Garlic (Chinese) chives | 100 g (3 1/2 oz), washed and cut into 3-cm (1 1/2-inch) lengths |
| Polygonum (*laksa*) leaves | 50 g (2 oz), washed and stems discarded |
| Fresh rice vermicelli | 1.5 kg (3 lb 4 1/2 oz) |
| Duck eggs | 2, fried into a thin omelette |
| Dried prawns (shrimps) | 150 g (5 1/3 oz), washed, drained and pounded until fine and pasty |
| Red chillies | 2, seeded and julienned |
| Skinned peanuts (groundnuts) | 30 g (1 oz), roasted and coarsely pounded |

**Step-By-Step**

Mix eel slices and seasoning ingredients well to ensure even infusion of flavours.

To make omelette, season beaten eggs with 1 pinch each of salt, pepper and seasoning powder, then fry. Julienne omelette.

Atop noodles, arrange egg shreds, minced pork and dried prawns in thirds, then place eel at the centre with some chilli slices.

### Method

- Fillet eel to debone (see pg 54). Reserve bones for stock (see pg 96), then slice eel fillets and set aside. Prepare stock.
- Season eel slices with 1/4 Tbsp each of garlic and spring onions, lemon grass, curry powder, 1 tsp each of salt and pepper, 2 tsp sugar and 2 Tbsp seasoning powder. Leave for 15 minutes.
- In another bowl, season pork with 1/4 Tbsp garlic, remaining spring onions salt, pepper, sugar and seasoning powder.
- Heat oil in a skillet (frying pan). Add remaining garlic and shallots. Fry until fragrant, then add eel and stir-fry until cooked through. Dish out.
- Dry-fry pork until cooked and dish out. Add prawn paste, if used, on top, but do not mix.
- Into individual serving bowls, put some bean sprouts and herbs, then vermicelli on top. Arrange prepared topping ingredients as shown, then ladle boiling soup over. Sprinkle on pounded peanuts and serve.

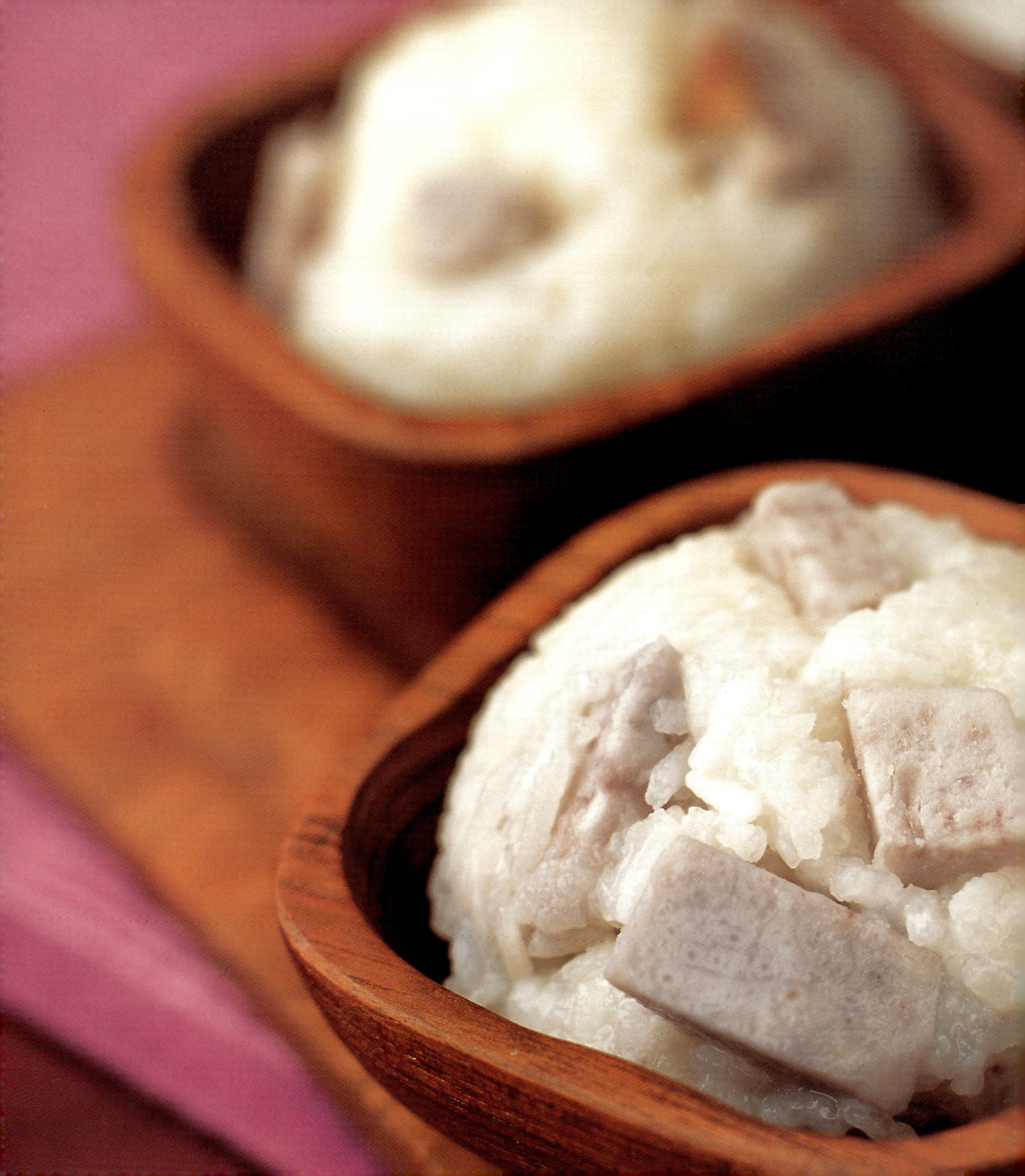

# DESSERTS

Peanut and Sago Dessert

Sweet Yam Dessert

Tapioca Cake

Fresh Aloe Vera with Green Bean Soup

Black-eyed Peas in Glutinous Rice

Soak peanuts in plenty of water and drain before use.

Tie screwpine leaves together into a knot for easier handling.

Add remaining ingredients only after the sago has turned clear or else the other ingredients could overcook.

*Step-By-Step*

# PEANUT AND SAGO DESSERT

With green beans, peanuts, sago and shredded black fungus, this dessert has a delightful variety of soft and crunchy textures.

### Ingredients

| | |
|---|---|
| Green (mung) beans | 300 g (10$^1$/$_2$ oz), soaked in water for 1 hour or until softened then rub off and discard skins |
| Peanuts (groundnuts) | 100 g (3$^1$/$_2$ oz), soaked in water for 1 hour and drained |
| Sugar | 200 g (7 oz) |
| Water | 2 litres (8 cups / 3$^1$/$_5$ pints) |
| Sago | 50 g (2 oz), soaked in water for 1 hour or until softened |
| Dried black (wood ear) fungus | 50 g (2 oz), soaked in water until soft then finely shred |
| Coconut cream | 200 ml (6$^1$/$_2$ fl oz) |
| Screwpine (*pandan*) leaves | 4, washed and dried, or $^1$/$_2$ tsp vanilla essence (extract) |
| Salt | $^1$/$_2$ tsp |

### Method

- Steam skinless green beans for about 5 minutes or until cooked through, but not soggy.
- Put peanuts in a pot. Add sufficient water to cover, then boil for about 20 minutes or until softened. Drain peanuts well, then transfer to a bowl. Add sugar and mix.
- Bring 2 litres (8 cups / 3$^1$/$_5$ pints) of water to the boil in a large pot. Add soaked sago and cook for 10 minutes or until sago becomes clear.
- Add all remaining ingredients and return to the boil, then turn off heat.
- Serve hot or cold.

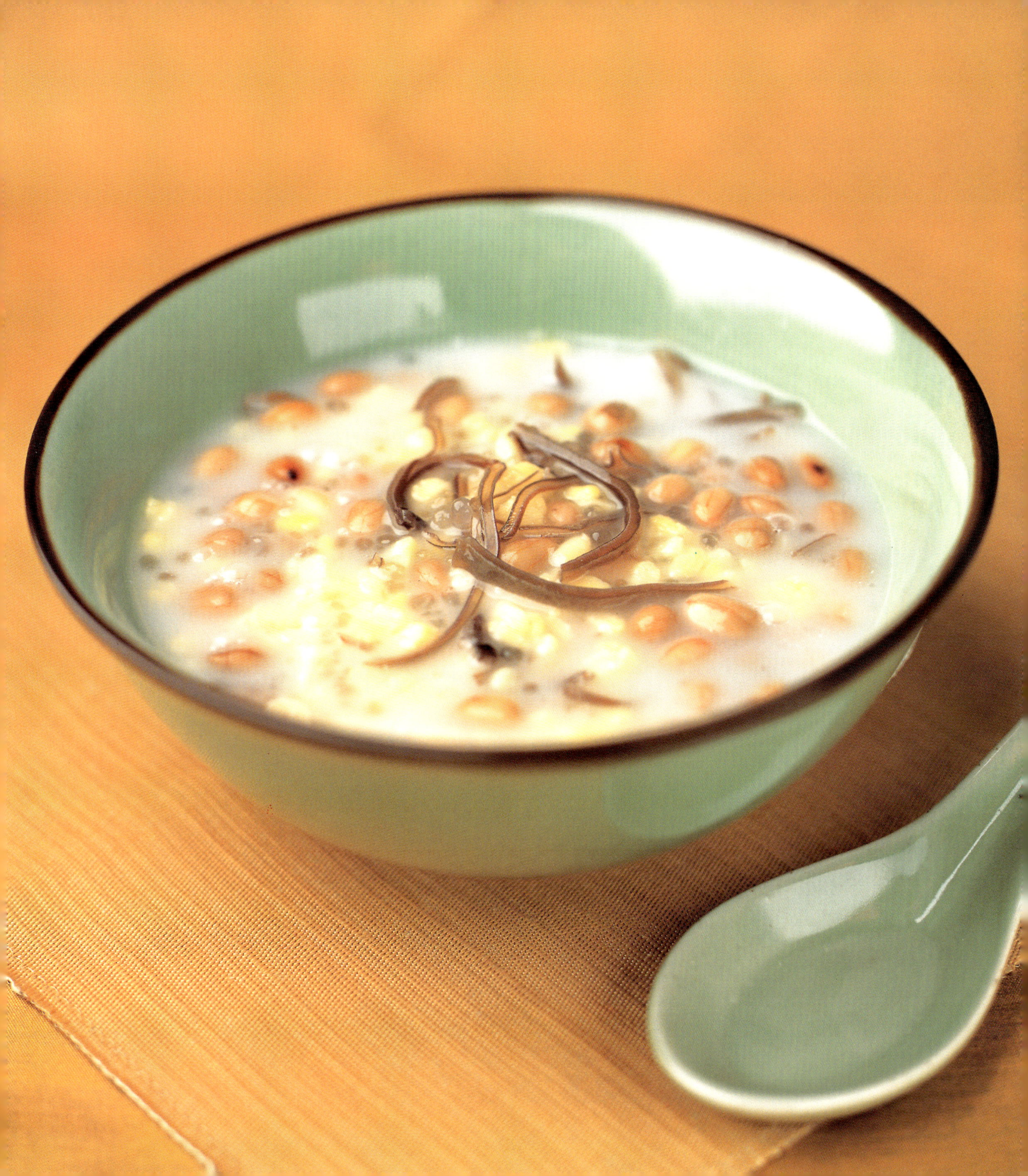

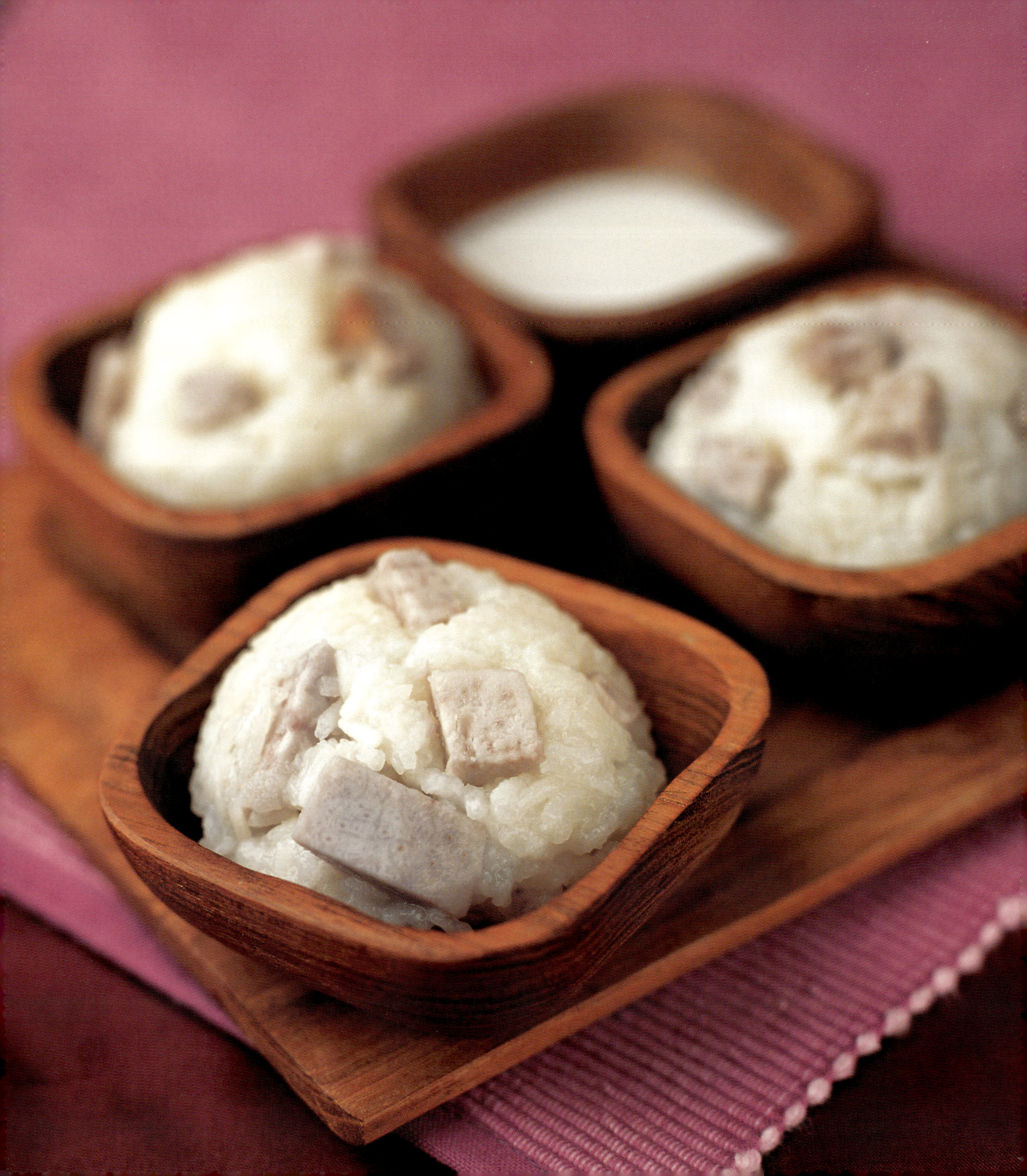

# SWEET YAM DESSERT

Similar to but starchier than the mango and sticky rice of Thai fame, this dessert is easy to prepare and a solid way to wrap up any meal.

### Ingredients

| | |
|---|---|
| Water | 2 litres (8 cups / 3 1/5 pints) |
| Glutinous rice | 250 g (9 oz), washed and soaked in water for 1–2 hours |
| Salt | 1/2 tsp |
| Sugar | 300 g (10 1/2 oz) |
| Yam (taro) | 500 g (1 lb 1 1/2 oz), washed, peeled and cut into bite-sized cubes |
| Screwpine (*pandan*) leaves | 4, washed, dried and tied together to form a bunch, or 1/2 tsp vanilla essence (extract) |
| Coconut milk | 300 ml (10 fl oz / 1 1/4 cup) |

**Step-By-Step**

Glutinous rice grains require much soaking before use. Otherwise, they take a long time to cook.

When the rice grains have absorbed the water until no liquid is visible from the top, add salt and half the sugar.

Mix in coconut milk when yam cubes are soft, which indicates that they are cooked through.

### Method

- Bring water to the boil. Add glutinous rice and cook for 20 minutes or until liquid is not visible from the top.
- Add salt and half the sugar. Cook until both are completely dissolved.
- Add yam, remaining sugar and screwpine leaves. Do not stir. Cook over low heat for 15 minutes or until yam cubes are cooked.
- Mix in coconut milk, then remove from heat and leave to cool. Serve in small bowls at room temperature.
- Alternatively, coconut milk can be served separately alongside dessert. Separately bring coconut milk to the boil, then add a solution of cornflour (cornstarch) and water to thicken.

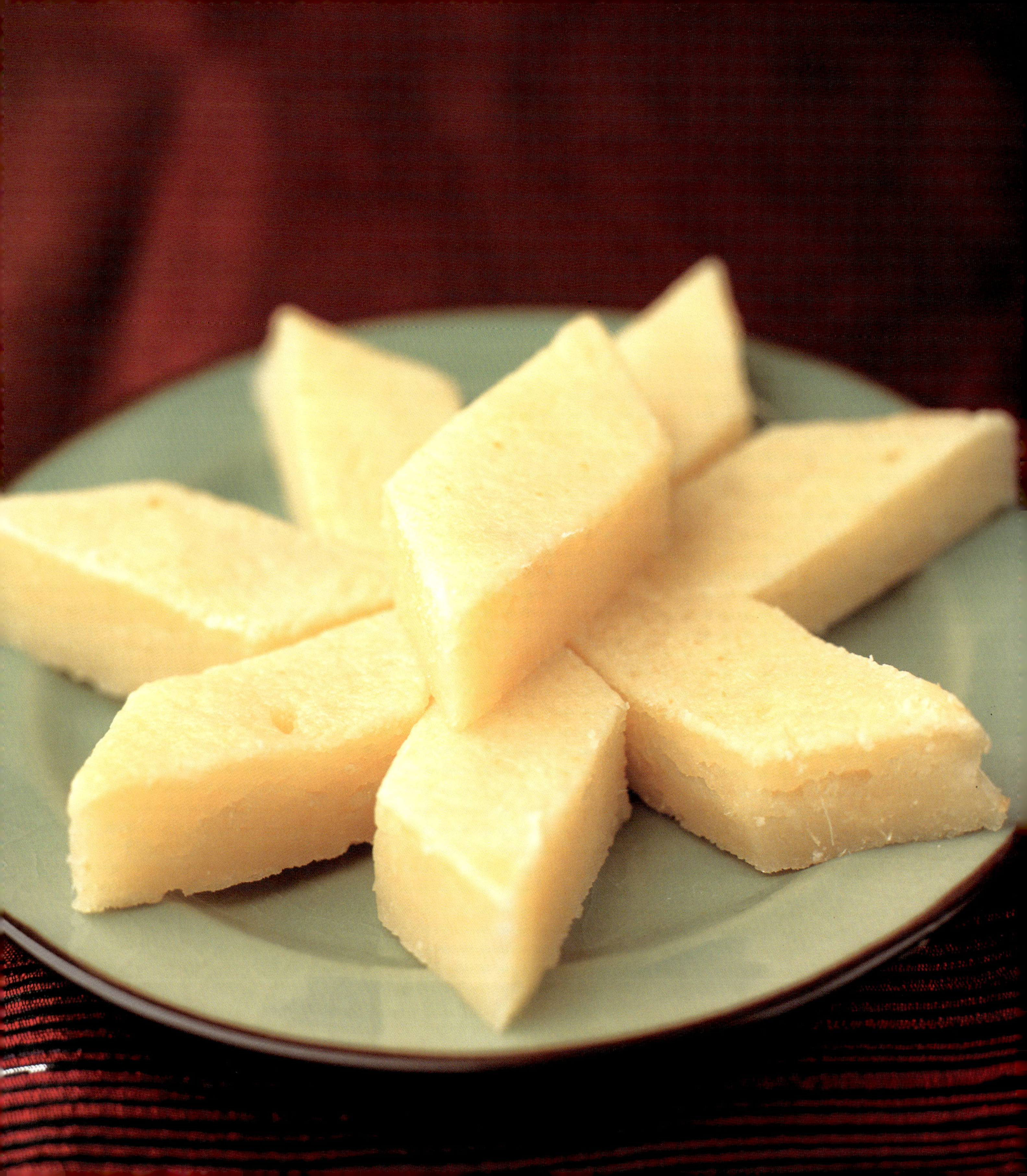

# TAPIOCA CAKE

As delicate as much of Vietnamese cuisine, this cake is mildly fragrant from the coconut cream and not overbearingly sweet.

### Ingredients

| | |
|---|---|
| Tapioca | 1 kg (2 lb 3 oz), washed, peeled and cut into small pieces then blended (processed) until fine and pasty |
| Coconut cream | 200 ml (6½ fl oz) |
| Condensed milk | 3 tsp |
| Vanilla essence (extract) | ½ tsp |
| Sugar | 100 g (3½ oz) |
| Salt | ½ tsp |
| Butter | 50 g (2 oz) |

**Step-By-Step**

Cut a ring around the tapioca root, then a straight line from the ring to one end. Hard brown skin peels away easily.

Using muslin cloth, squeeze blended or processed tapioca to remove excess liquid.

Melt butter in a non-stick pan so that burning and wastage are minimised.

### Method

- Put tapioca paste into a cloth bag or fine strainer. Squeeze firmly to drain out excess liquid. Use about 650 g (1 lb 6½ oz) of tapioca paste to make cake. Reserve and refrigerate any remainder for future use.
- Put tapioca paste into a large bowl. Mix in coconut cream, condensed milk, vanilla essence, sugar, salt and half the butter.
- Melt remaining butter and use it to grease the base of a 20–25 cm (8–10-inch) round metal cake tin.
- Bake in oven preheated to 180°C/350°F for about 15 minutes or until surface is golden brown.
- Remove cake from oven and leave to cool. Turn out cooled cake, then slice and serve.

If available, use fresh lotus seeds instead of dried. They do not require soaking and cook in much less time.

If very large, aloe vera should be cut into shorter segments for easier handling.

Add sugar only when lotus seeds and green beans are cooked through and soft.

*Step-By-Step*

# FRESH ALOE VERA WITH GREEN BEAN SOUP

Cooked aloe vera may not taste of very much, but they leave a lightly tangy after-taste that is refreshing and welcome to a laden palate.

### Ingredients
| | |
|---|---|
| Split green (mung) beans | 300 g (10½ oz), leave skins on if attached |
| Dried lotus seeds (optional) | 100 g (3½ oz), or fresh ones if available |
| Water | 1.5 litres (6 cups / 2⅖ pints) |
| Sugar | 100 g (3½ oz) or to taste |
| Aloe vera leaves | 2, peeled and sliced or cubed |

### Method

- Soak green beans in water for 2 hours and drain before use. Do not discard skins if available.
- Soak dried lotus seeds in water for 2 hours and drain before use. Fresh lotus seeds do not need soaking.
- Boil soaked lotus seeds, if used, in plenty of water until soft, then drain. Fresh lotus seeds do not need boiling.
- Combine lotus seeds, green beans and 1.5 litres (6 cups / 2⅖ pints) water in a pot. Cook for about 20 minutes.
- Add sugar to taste. When satisfied, add aloe vera pieces and remove from heat.

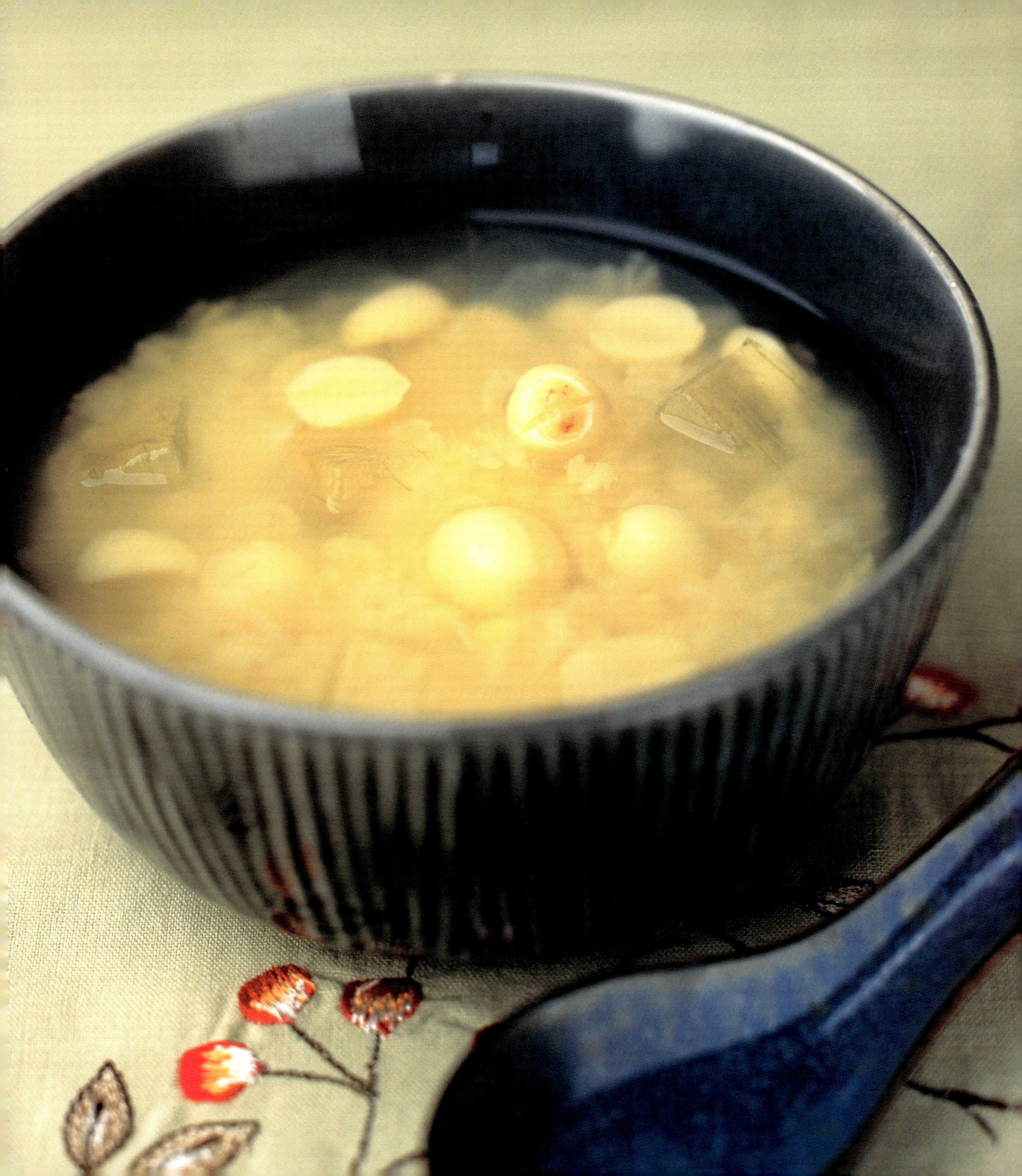

Dried black-eyes peas require much soaking before use, so do plan ahead.

Bring black-eyed peas, 1 litre (4 cups / 1 3/5 pints) water and bicarbonate of soda, which helps to soften the peas, to the boil.

Add black-eyed peas when rice grains have absorbed most of the water in which they were cooked.

*Step-By-Step*

# BLACK-EYED PEAS IN GLUTINOUS RICE

Another filling end to a meal, this substantial dessert is flavoured by a fragrant combination of coconut milk and vanilla essence.

### Ingredients

| | |
|---|---|
| Black-eyed peas | 300 g (10 1/2 oz), soaked in cold water for 3 hours, then drained |
| Bicarbonate of (baking) soda | 1 tsp |
| Water | 1.75 litres (7 cups / 2 4/5 pints) |
| Glutinous rice | 250 g (9 oz) |
| Sugar | 350 g (12 1/2 oz) |
| Coconut milk | 125 ml (4 fl oz / 1/2 cup) |
| Vanilla essence (extract) | 1/2 tsp |

### Method

- Combine peas, bicarbonate of soda and 1 litre (4 cups / 1 3/5 pints) water in a pot. Bring to the boil and sustain for about 1 hour. Do not over-boil.
- When peas are soft, but not broken, remove from heat, drain and set aside.
- Rinse rice grains twice. Cook rice in remaining water over low heat for about 45 minutes, stirring frequently.
- When rice liquid is mostly evaporated, add boiled peas and cook for 20 minutes.
- Add remaining ingredients, mix well and cook for 20 minutes more.
- When dessert is thickened and consistent in texture, remove from heat.

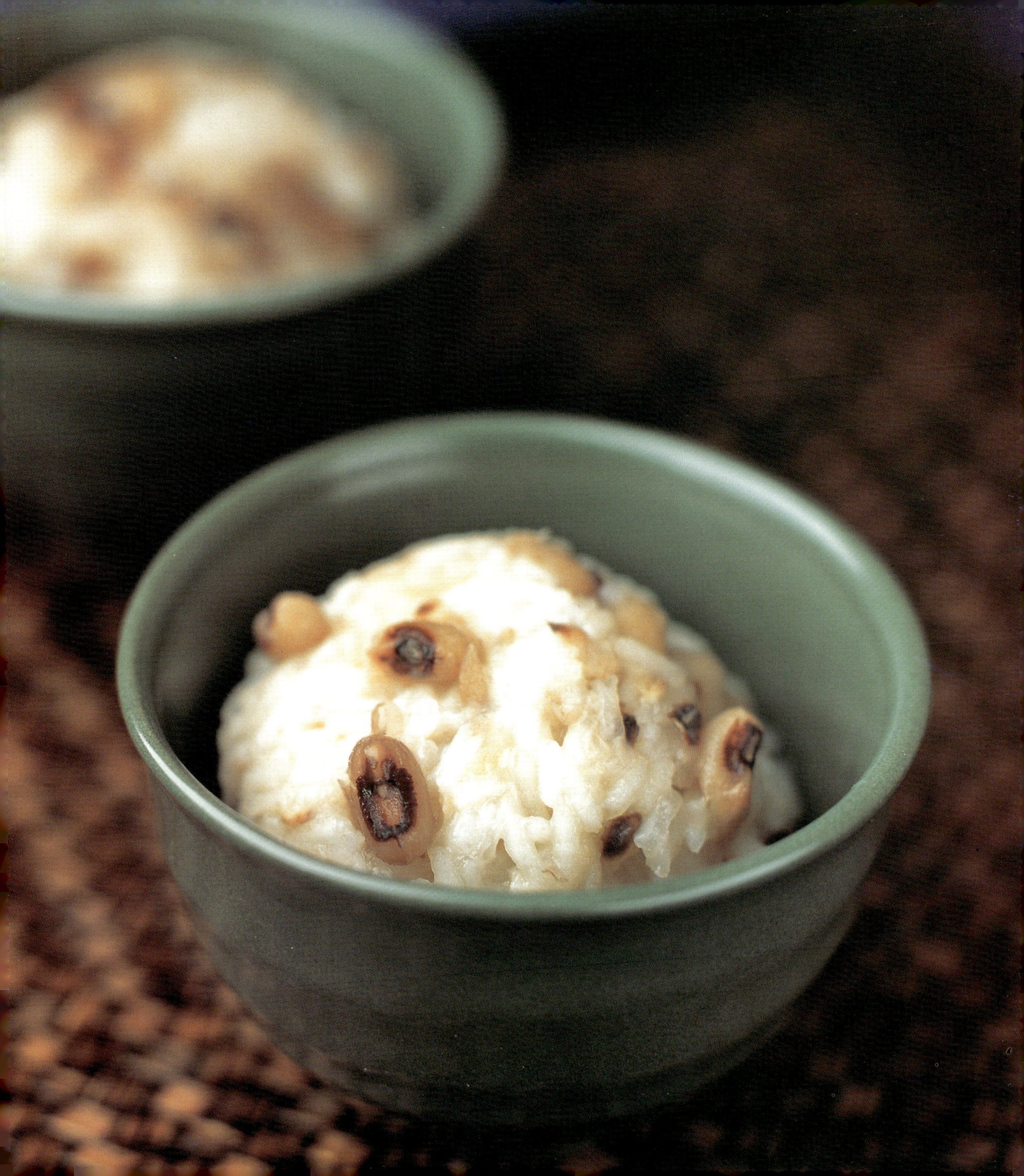

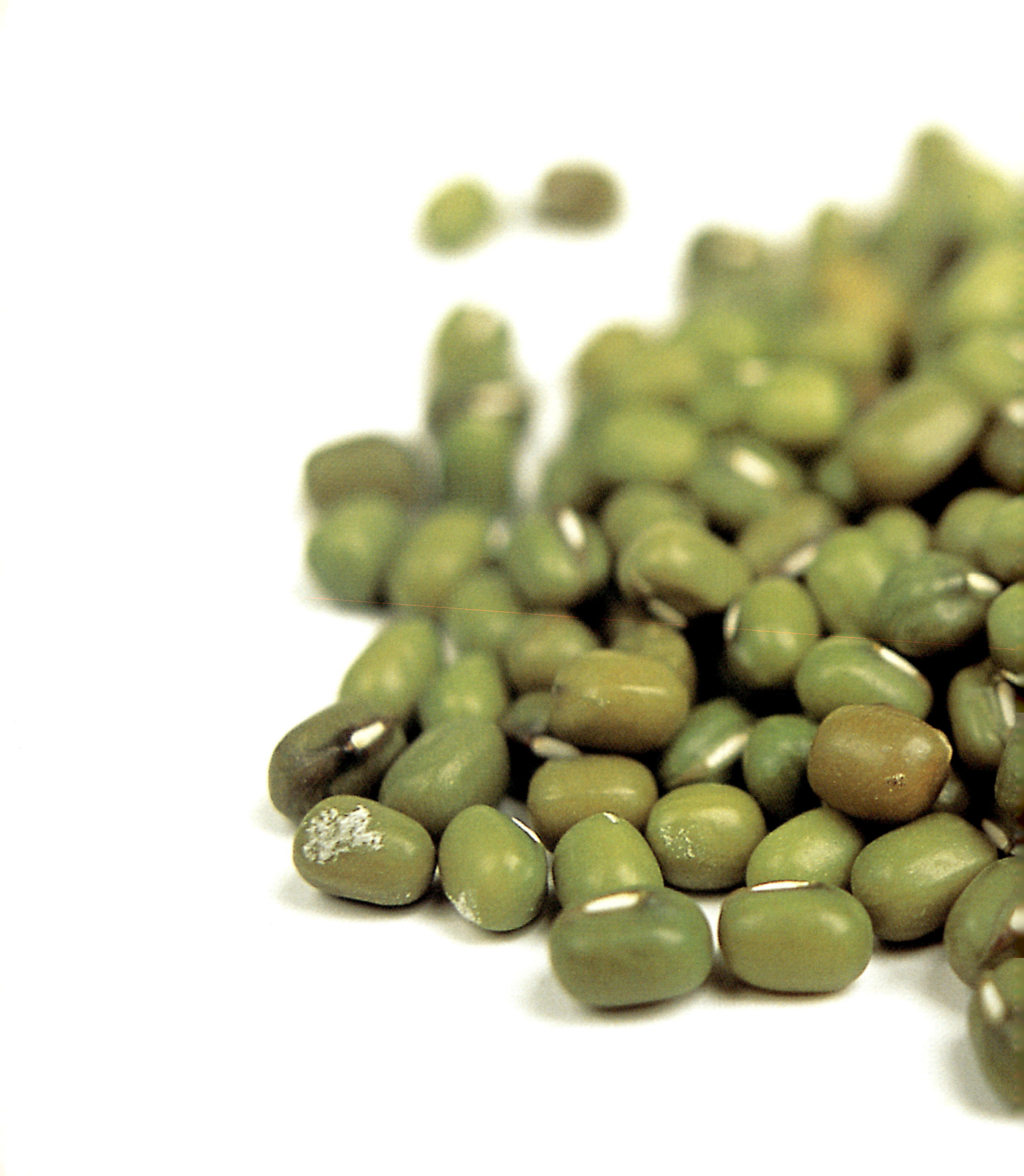

Glossary of Ingredients

Index

# GLOSSARY & INDEX

# GLOSSARY OF INGREDIENTS

### Bird's Eye Chillies
Never underestimate bird's eye chillies because they are tiny. Within each one are seeds that appear like white specks. These specks are potent and impart a fiery spiciness that will scorch unsuspecting mouths and tongues to the point of tears. Red chillies that look like much larger versions of bird's eye chillies are also much milder.

### Black (Wood Ear) Fungus
Hard, curly-edged pieces of dried fungus expand astonishingly with soaking. Almost invariably, first-time users will overestimate the amount they soak to derive what they really need. Should that happen, drain the soaked fungus of water well and store in a covered container in the refrigerator. It will keep comfortably for up to a week.

### Chinese Cabbage
Also known as napa cabbage, elongated heads of Chinese cabbage consist of tightly packed leaves, each of which are frilly and a very faint green along the edges and at the centre is a wide white, ridged stem.

### Chinese Lettuce
Also known as leaf or curled lettuce, Chinese lettuce comes in small bunches resembling bouquets. Although iceberg lettuce leaves can be a substitute, Chinese lettuce leaves are said to have a higher nutritional value than those of iceberg lettuce simply because of their darker, rich green colour.

### Coconut Juice
Not to be confused with coconut milk or cream, coconut juice is the clear liquid found inside a coconut and a refreshing drink on a hot day. Coconut milk and cream are white in colour and they are derived from squeezing the grated flesh of the coconut. Coconut cream, then, is also known as No.1 or thick coconut milk, which is produced when grated coconut flesh is squeezed using muslin cloth with little to no water added. Coconut milk is sometimes called No.2 or thin coconut milk, which is derived by squeezing the same grated coconut a second time with water added.

### Coriander (Cilantro) Leaves
A strongly aromatic herb, coriander is also known as Chinese parsley. The plant's leaves are often used as garnishing, while its stems and root are more widely used to impart flavour and fragrance, especially to liquid-based dishes. Not to be confused with Chinese celery, which looks very similar but has larger leaves and juicier, stiffer stems.

### Crisp-fried Shallots
Thin shallot slices turn into brown crispy curls when fried in oil. These crisp-fried shallots are often used as garnishing over noodles in soup, congee or even stir-fries, where they provide added flavour and an appetising aroma.

### Dried Prawns (Shrimps)
Peeled small prawns are salted and then dried. Tiny but pungent, dried prawns are used in many Southeast Asian cuisines. They make a fiesty flavouring agent and only small amounts need to be used each time. Dried prawns need to be soaked in water to soften and drained before use. Apart from softening, the process also helps to remove excess salt and impurities.

### Fermented Prawn (Shrimp) Paste
Not to be confused with another type of fermented prawn paste that is black and also common in Asian cooking, this prawn paste is arguably mauve in colour and pasty in texture, somewhat like mashed chickpeas or potatoes. The black fermented prawn paste is thick and gooey, more like a thick syrup or liquid glue.

### Fish Sauce
Vietnamese fish sauce may be similar enough to Thai fish sauce in the larger scheme of things but is nevertheless quite distinct in taste. Vietnamese fish sauce is said to be more tangy than its Thai counterpart, which is more salty. For the uninitiated, fish sauce can be unpalatably fishy, although this is sometimes also a question of quality. Generally, better quality products are less fishy. The fishiness of fish sauce can be tempered with any or a combination of the following: lime juice, vinegar or sugar. In fact, simply diluting the sauce with some water often helps. When a recipe calls for a considerable amount of fish sauce, add it to the dish in small amounts, adjusting it to taste as you go. It is far more problematic to counter the effects of too much fish sauce in a given dish.

### Glutinous Rice
Also known as sticky rice, glutinous rice is of a solid pearl white colour. The rice grains require at least 2 hours of soaking before use and, when cooked, become translucent and sticky, hence the name. In Asian cuisines, glutinous rice is used as a staple and also to make many desserts. Glutinous rice is considerably denser than regular steamed rice, so portions should be reduced if cooking for a staple. There is a variety of black glutinous rice.

### Green (Mung) Beans
Green beans are the sources of bean sprouts commonly seen in Asian cooking. Green beans are most often bought whole and dried, which means that they require soaking before use. The skins of the beans loosen with soaking and some people discard these skins, while others do not in view of their nutritional value. Green beans can also be bought skinless and split. Without their outer covering, green beans are a bright light yellow and cook easily. In other words, they are likely to disintegrate with prolonged boiling.

### Lemon Grass
These pale yellow stalks impart a faint lemony fragrance to dishes. The leaves of lemon grass are very fibrous and usually require mincing in order to use. The lower, more bulbous part can be either minced or simply bruised with the handle or back of a knife to release the fragrance, depending on the requirements of the dish at hand. In a curry or a liquid-based dish, for example, bruising will suffice. If the lemon grass is part of a marinade, however, then mincing is advised.

### Lotus Seeds
Dried lotus seeds require considerable preparation before use. For a start, they will need to be soaked in water for some hours or quickly parboiled to slightly soften. Then, the brown skins and the green cores, which are bitter, need to be removed, if either or both are attached. While the brown skins can be simply rubbed off, there are two ways to remove the green cores — either split each seed in two and brush it off or poke a bamboo toothpick or cocktail stick through the centre of the seed to push the core out. The latter method has the advantage of leaving the seeds whole. In recent years, however, fresh, skinless lotus seeds have become available in some supermarkets. Although they, too, have the green cores attached, they require no soaking or parboiling before use. Canned lotus seeds may need the least preparation but their mushy softness leaves much to be desired.

### Polygonum (Laksa) Leaves
Polygonum leaves is also known as Vietnamese mint and they impart a strong and unique herby flavour. These leaves are indispensable to a dish called *laksa* that is popular in Singapore and Malaysia, so much so that they are also known as *laksa* leaves to some suppliers.

### Prawn (Shrimp) Crackers
Raw prawn crackers are hard, dense and irregularly shaped discs that take on a charming transformation when lowered into hot oil — first sinking to the bottom, then seemingly blossoming and surfacing. The light and crispy fried products (*left*) have been well-loved as snacks for generations in Asia.

### Red Fermented Bean Curd
Fermented bean curd comes in two main types: white and red. The white variety is usually served and eaten alongside plain rice or congee, while the red variety is more commonly cooked and used to flavour dishes. These knobs of bean curd fermented in rice wine are pungent and can be an acquired taste. In fact, fermented bean curd pieces are so strong-smelling and -tasting that they are also known as bean curd cheese.

### Rice Vermicelli
Rice vermicelli is most commonly available dried, although some Asian markets sell them fresh. Fresh rice vermicelli has a sticky quality that the dried variety, even after reconstitution, does not possess. If the fresh rice vermicelli is required in a roll or in a dish where its stickiness is required, then it is advisable to substitute with Indian string hoppers (*putu mayam*) or thick round rice (*laksa*) noodles. In the event that the fresh rice vermicelli is meant for a noodle dish, then dried rice vermicelli can be substituted. The rule of thumb is to quarter the weight of fresh vermicelli called for in a recipe and then let that figure be the amount of dried vermicelli required for reconstituting.

### Preserved Soy Beans
Preserved soy beans are sometimes called fermented soy beans. They are salty and have a distinct taste, and are most often used in making sauces or marinades. Preserved soy beans are usually sold in jars and in different forms — whole beans, paste or half-and-half, which is a mixture of split beans and paste. Whole beans tend to be hard and require blending (processing) before use. While the ready-made paste is the most convenient to use, it is also the most costly. The beans in half-and-half are softer than whole beans and can be mashed to moderate fineness with the back of a spoon.

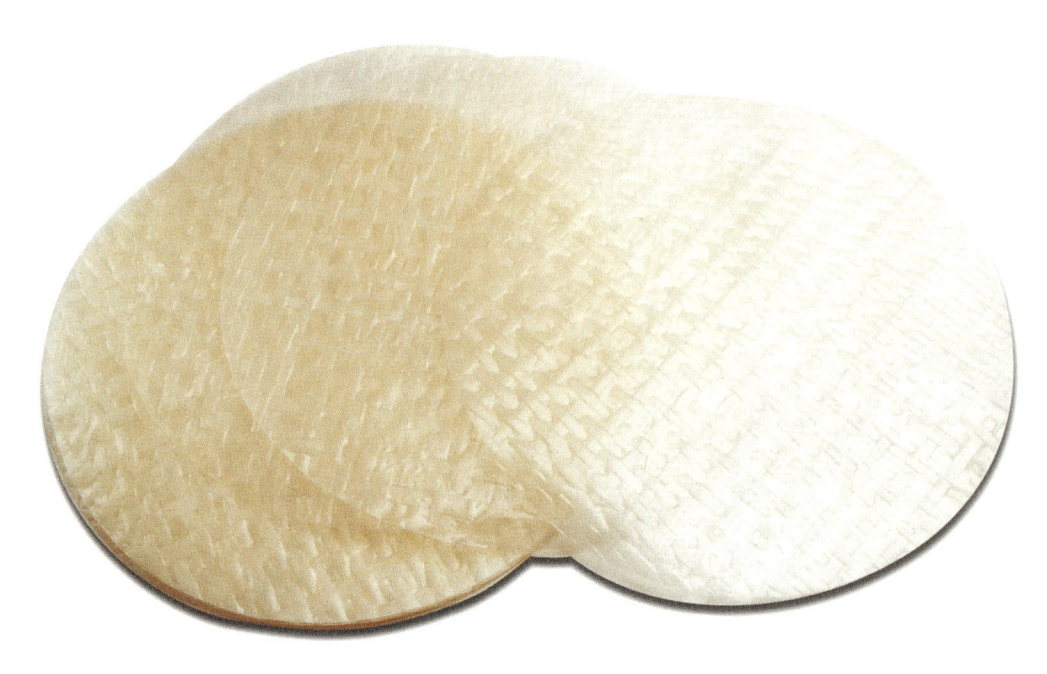

### Round Rice Papers
A quintessentially Vietnamese condiment, round rice papers are sold as dried, white discs sealed in plastic packets. The rice papers need to be softened with water before use. Liquid turns the white discs into translucent sticky sheets that require careful handling, an experience similar to trying to use overly sticky cling film (plastic wrap) or to undoing a long, mangled strip of sticky tape. The rice papers, however, are remarkably resistant to tears even when dampened.

### Sago
Sago comes from the sago palm, an evergreen plant native to Asia. Store bought sago comes in the form of tiny, white balls, but they expand and become transparent when cooked. Cooked sago also has a squishy texture that works well with many liquid-based desserts.

### Screwpine Leaves
Commonly known in Southeast Asia as *pandan* leaves, screwpine leaves impart a unique and subtle fragrance that somehow makes a world of difference in lifting the dish, usually desserts, out of stodginess. The leaves are usually washed and knotted together before use. Most times, a knot of 5–6 leaves will suffice in scenting a stock pot of ingredients, although the amount can be increased or decreased to taste.

### Soft Bean Curd
The general tastelessness of bean curd is also the reason for its great adaptability. It will readily absorb the flavours of any dish to which it has been added. Soft bean curd, while requiring some care in handling, is also more versatile than other, harder forms of bean curd. Pieces of soft bean curd, for example, can be deep-fried in hot oil for a more interesting texture, resulting in a brown crispy skin on the outside while remaining custard soft inside. Alternatively, soft bean curd can be mashed into little bits to combine with other ingredients.

### Spring Onions (Scallions)
Spring onions are usually divided into two parts to serve different purposes in Asian cooking. The green leaves readily collapse with heat and are more often used for garnishing, while the hard, white stalks tend to be cooked. Spring onions in general impart a light onion-like zing, while the stalks also provide some crunch.

### Straw Mushrooms
Unlike mushrooms typically used in Asian cooking, such as Chinese or shiitake, straw mushrooms are relatively bland, which allows them to take on the dominant flavours of the dish to which they have been added. They, as is the case with other mushrooms, are a great source of minerals and nutrients.

### Thin Flat Rice Noodles
Sold fresh or dried, these noodles arguably can be described as a rice version of fettucini, only slightly thinner. In most instances, they are available dried and in bundles, these noodles need to be soaked to soften before use. Alternatively, they can be blanched in hot water. The latter method, however, requires some skill or else the noodles can disintegrate from over-cooking, which can be prevented by lowering the blanched noodles into a basin of cold water or rinsing gently under a running tap. These noodles work well in a soup or stir-fried.

### Transparent (Glass) Vermicelli
Made from green (mung) bean flour, transparent vermicelli is sold dried in plastic packets. The noodles become transparent with cooking, which explains their name. Transparent vermicelli is generally more springy than that made of rice and adds great texture and crunch to a dish.

### Taro (Yam)
A starchy root that Asians generally also know as yam, taro is used in both dishes and desserts. Taro has the texture of potato when cooked, but possesses a nuttier flavour.

### Watercress
A pungent-tasting vegetable, not unlike rocket (arugula) leaves, watercress works well in conjunction with other ingredients with forward flavours. Delicate tastes and aromas are likely to be lost alongside watercress.

# INDEX

**A**
alcohol  24, 43, 78

**B**
Baked Crabs  49
Beef Cooked in Vinegar  72
Beef Noodles  85
Beef on Fire  70
Beef Rolls  24
Beef Salad  40
Black-eyed Peas in Glutinous
   Rice  108

**C**
Chinese lettuce  16, 19, 21, 24, 28,
   70, 72
Chicken Salad with Polygonum
   Leaves  43
cilantro *see* coriander
coconut cream  100, 105
coconut juice  16, 19, 21, 22, 24,
   28, 37, 38, 40, 46, 51, 69, 70,
   72, 77
coconut milk  35, 78, 90, 103, 108
coriander  40, 52, 64, 78
Crabmeat Noodle Soup  88

**D**
Deep-fried Spring Rolls  19
Duck Cooked in Fermented Bean
   Curd  90
Duck Noodle Soup  87

**E**
Eel Noodles  97

**F**
fish  32, 46, 51, 52, 54
Fish and Pineapple Stew  46
Fresh Aloe Vera with Green Bean
   Soup  106
Fresh Spring Rolls  16
Fried Chicken Wings in Fish
   Sauce  26
Fried Crab in Tamarind Sauce  57
Fried Lemon Grass Chicken  64

**G**
Green Mango Salad  37

**H**
Hanoi Prawn Fritters  21

**L**
lemon grass  16, 54, 64, 69, 70, 72,
   78, 97

**P**
peanuts  16, 37, 38, 40, 54, 70, 78,
   87, 95, 97, 100
Peanut and Sago Dessert  100
Pork Stewed in Coconut Juice  77
prawn  16, 21, 22, 35, 37, 38, 59,
   60, 95
Prawn Paste on Sugar Cane  22
Prawns Sautéed with Pork Belly  59
Pumpkin Soup with Coconut
   Milk  35

**Q**
Quang Noodles  95

**R**
rolls  16, 19, 24, 70, 72, 51

## S

Saigon Fish Congee 93
shrimp *see* prawn
Squid Cakes 28
Steamed Chicken with Spring Onions 67
Steamed Fish with Fermented Soy Beans 52
Steamed Fish with Sugar Cane 51
Steamed Minced Pork with Duck Eggs 75
Stir-fried Frog in Coconut Milk 78
Stir-fried Minced Eel with Lemon Grass 54
Stuffed Squid 60
Sweet Yam Dessert 103

## T

tamarind 32, 57
Tapioca Cake 105
Traditional Chicken Noodle Soup 82

## V

Vietnamese Sour Fish Soup 32
Vietnamese Beef Stew 69

## W

Water Convolvulus Salad 38